Awakened By The Flowers

with Channeled Messages and Watercolor Mandalas

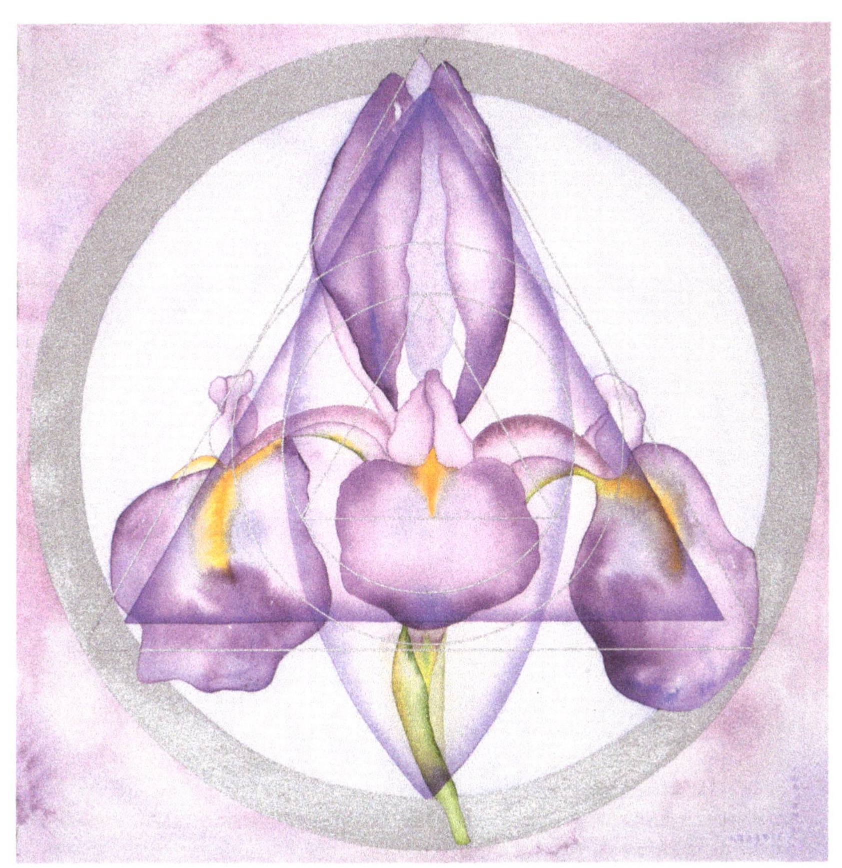

Michele Faia

www.michelefaia.com

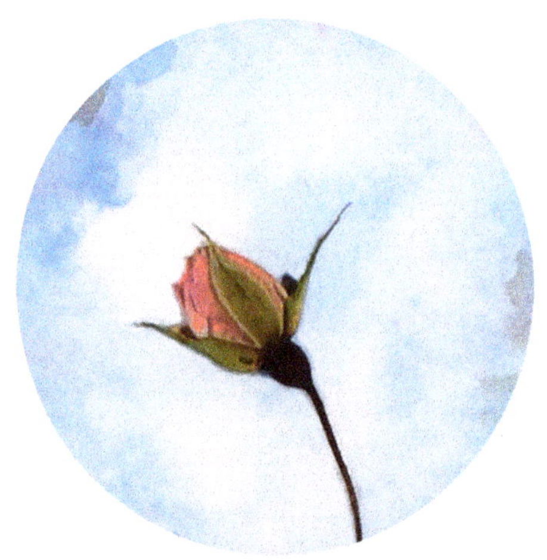

Awakened by the Flowers
With Channeled Messages and Watercolor Mandalas
Michele Faia – 1st Edition
Third Printing 2021

Published by Michele Faia
Aptos, CA
Copyright ©2016

Awakened by the Flowers describes the personal experiences
of the author and reflects her views. It is not intended as a guide
to personal diagnosis or independent medical self-healing.
No medical claim is made as to the effect of the
exercises described in this book.

Creative Direction and Design: Don Faia
Front Cover Art: *Iris and Triangle*, Michele Faia
Formatting and Production : Anita Bonno Bernard

ISBN # 9-780692-761052

TABLE OF CONTENTS

FORWARD

There are several ways to approach this book to get the most out of it. First, just enjoy looking at the pictures! You'll get a lot just from that—the paintings are full of energy and I still get energized when I simply hold the book. Thumb through it and read a bit here and there. Look at it with the eyes of your heart and see what speaks to you. Can you begin to open to the possibility of color's subtle energies and light? Color is subtle but powerful. If you want to go deeper, find a quiet place where you can start to read the book and allow yourself to relax into the messages. Take your time. Notice how they make you feel and the affect they have on you. I would then encourage you to try the exercises themselves. I found them quite powerful, enlightening, soothing and full of love. Whatever your approach to the book, relax and enjoy it. My hope is that it makes you smile, inspires you to try something new for yourself and gives you pleasure. Maybe you'll see color in a new way, or stop and really look at flowers. Maybe you'll take that art class you've always wanted to try. Perhaps you have been wanting to contact your spirit guides, and you decide to give it a go. The possibilities are endless. Above all, have fun!

I have been asked many times, "How do you channel?" For me it starts with a knowing that I need to pay attention to a kind of profoundness that begins to surround me. I can feel there is a higher energy that comes over me, which is clearly not from my own chattering mind. It's wonderful, it feels good. I love connecting with spirit this way. I've always written down what I receive rather than speaking it out loud. Usually, at first, there is a word or even a color which comes through strongly, and if I can grab ahold of that, I'm on my way. It's like plugging in, making the connection. I feel so wonderful when the message is complete. I know I have connected with a higher wisdom and I feel blissful for a time. There is a history of God, or the angels, speaking to mortals, especially in the Bible. It's really nothing new, but it may be new for you personally. For many years I had studied with a woman who channeled, and have tended to enjoy channeled material in books, not all of it, but some. So I was familiar with the concept of receiving messages. I've always been careful about what I read, or who I listen to. It has to be from the light. That's how it all started for me, with seeing the light within myself in meditation. I encourage you to try. Remember, all you have to do is ask. Surround yourself in light, ask and then listen. Your spirit guides have been waiting for your invitation. And, with that simple connection, be ready to receive such love, blessings and to feel such gratitude!

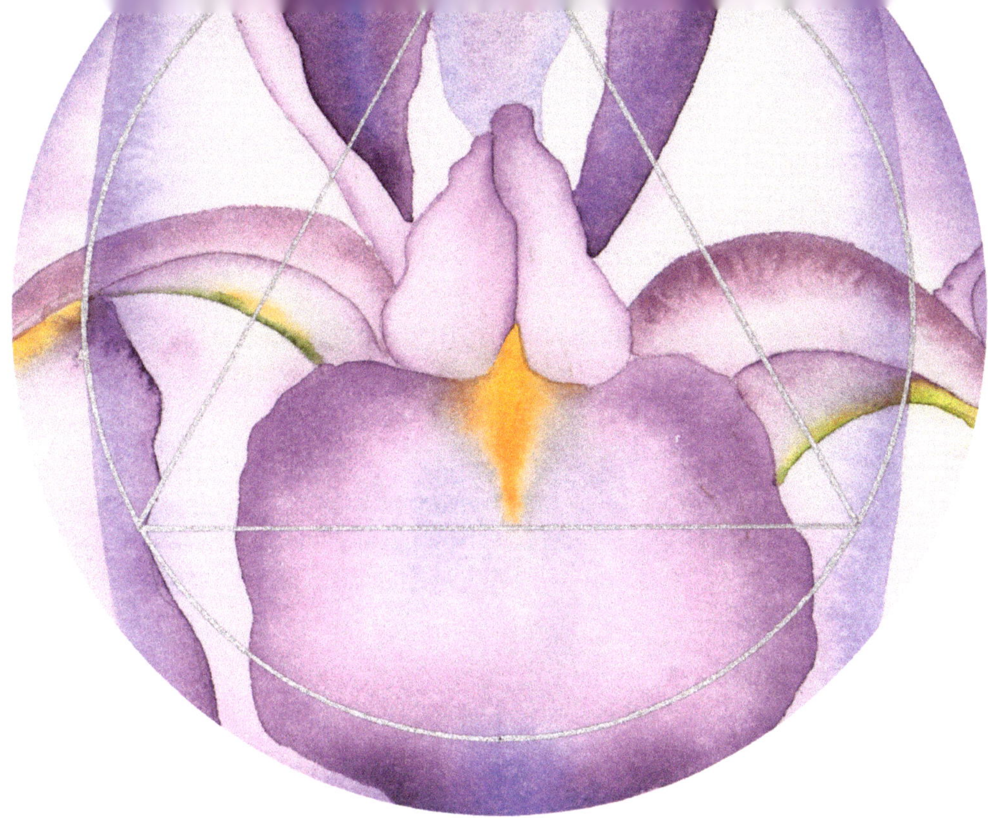

Waking Up With Color, Flowers & Messages

This book is about waking up, which is especially challenging when you didn't know you were asleep. My story, although written by me, is unusual in the sense that the words are from my spirit guides. They came as inspired messages which I heard within myself and transcribed, from my guides, who encouraged me to follow my heart and find my true inner work. That gave me the courage to do what I loved, which was to paint from my heart and soul, and what I painted was mostly flowers. It has definitely been an eye-opening journey, during which I learned who I was as a spiritual being, as well as finally accepting myself as an artist. As if that wasn't enough, I learned much about light, color and healing from a very different perspective and in a most unusual way. It certainly was not what I thought I'd be doing in my life, and I did wonder sometimes if it was real or if I was making the whole thing up. But I trusted and did what I was encouraged to do. In the end my story is not so different from others who are struggling to find their creative voices. As an instructor, I have seen so many souls like mine, searching for heart-centered personal artistic expression as we rise out of the depths of self-doubt. We truly are everywhere. This book is for all of us.

My Story

Essentially my story is told with watercolor mandalas and messages from my spirit guides. And, when all is said and done, it's really the story of how art saved me. Mandalas have been a powerful healing tool for me for many years. I first painted them when I was ill and not able to work. My guides called my mandalas "Flower Energy Paintings." They would have "the ability to heal," they said, "because they carry the love of God. " In this book the mandalas are married with information from my guides, written "with purity and from spirit," and channeled over a number of years. From the very beginning, the first messages I received were for me to realize that spirit was always with me, loved me and that I could ask for and receive help at any time. My primary work, according to my guides, was about color and its power to awaken, open the heart and heal. I learned this in my garden while being with my flowers as I was both encouraged to do by my guides and loved doing. This was reinforced by messages I got directly from flowers, in the form of poetry, which was certainly new and different for me. So, along with my mandalas in the book are stories of transformation as I opened up to the spiritual guidance which was being presented to me. After getting messages of love and support for a long time, little by little I began taking them to heart, believing them, believing in myself, and watching all of that transform my life. I was being guided through a spiritual awakening as my life, my work and my art moved in a spiritual direction. I was becoming aware of what could be called my spiritual calling: to be with my flowers and paint, to become open and heal with color and to share that and the light with others. But, I was told, this story is not just about me. It is about all of us and what can be accomplished with the help of spirit. Anyone can do it—ask for and get help for oneself, and awaken to one's own spiritual calling.

In retrospect, art, spirituality and flowers have defined my life. It was all in my blood, from my grandfathers who started out as artist/craftsmen, to my great-grandfather who ministered around the country on horseback, to my grandmother whose traditional religion I found comforting as a child. I also found the gardens my parents grew very comforting. My father's vegetable garden fed our family and the neighborhood and my mother's beautiful flowers provided joy to others. From her I learned to love flowers and from my dad, to grow things.

I always liked art as a child. Well, it was more than that. I loved it. But being very sensitive, I feared criticism and doing something "wrong" and struggled with that most of my life. My artistic endeavors went underground.

I had one great teacher who encouraged me in art, but mostly I stayed under the radar and away from any criticism in school because I was so afraid of it. In college I majored in art history, not art, because I thought I was not good enough to pursue art as a career. Upon graduation I taught art history at a community college for a short time but left and got a job in public relations. I was haunted, however, by my love of art and questioned where it belonged in my life.

I began going to meditation classes with a former student. The classes were taught by a woman named Hope. She was a channel who received wonderful channeled messages, and I attended her light group for about six or seven years. It was there that I saw the light within myself in my first meditation and I was hooked—I wanted more of this. In Hope's weekly classes we were taught about light and its power, and that we were all teachers of the light.

It was during this time I learned that St. Germaine was my spiritual teacher and guide. That was exciting and a whole new part of my life opened up. (See Part IV.) In the public relations job I met an artist/graphic designer, who came in to show me his portfolio, and it was practically love at first sight. It was then that I began to draw and paint from the innermost place in my heart for the first time in my life. Of course, it certainly didn't hurt that this man liked my art and gave me more encouragement than I ever had before.

I married the graphic designer, we bought a house and I left my job and worked in odd jobs so I could quietly pursue my personal, artistic expression. Thank God for my husband's understanding and support! I continued to struggle with whether or not this was the right thing to do and eventually got very ill over the stress it caused. It was at this time that I started receiving messages from my spirit guides. I didn't see the significance of that at the time, but it was all part of the help I needed to change directions— from focusing on the outer life, to focusing on the inner one. It was going to be a "new venture," my guides told me. The truth was, I really wanted to paint from my own inner self.

After many years of going to doctors to find out why I was so ill, I was diagnosed with CFS, Chronic Fatigue Syndrome, an autoimmune disease. I had begun to paint mandalas, or sacred circles, drawn to them I believe for their healing qualities which acted on emotional, physical and spiritual levels. With encouragement from my guides, I returned to teaching, this time showing others how to paint mandalas, all from my own experience. I began to heal. With the inner work I was doing by painting my personal mandalas, and a good doctor, I eventually began to have more and more good days. I painted many mandalas and taught numerous classes. I wrote my first book, *Art in My Heart; The Power of Watercolor Mandala Making*, based on the technique I developed for teaching how to paint mandalas. The power of the mandala process was profound and I saw many students touch into their creativity and inner spirit. I witnessed a lot of healing, including my own. This book came out of that process, and with it the healing continued, all under the direction of my teachers and guides in spirit.

About This Book

For years I had been receiving messages from my spirit guides which I "heard" within my inner self and wrote down. I got the first one in 1977 from "Sara" while sitting in the beautiful lit-tle church where my husband was baptized. I didn't receive any messages or pick up a pen and paper to write anything again for ten years. Then in 1987 I began to get messages regularly and was encouraged by a spiritual teacher I had at the time to write them down, date and save them. What I received was usually in response to something I wanted to know about my own spiritual growth. Sometimes I would ask questions and get answers, and sometimes answers would come to questions I hadn't yet formulated. They came as an urge to sit and write, and when I did, the words would flow very easily. The messages were usually just for me and offered the help I needed. Therefore it did surprise me, when on a morning walk I heard from within the announcement: "We are going to write a book together." After I got home that day, I received a long message from St. Germaine who said we would write a book about the power of color. He suggested that I continue the work I was doing with flowers (I grew them and was experimenting with painting their spiritual energy,) and use the flowers to learn about color and energy. It was he who called my mandalas "Flower Energy Paintings," with the ability to heal. The information for the book would come from spirit, he said, so I began to watch for the tap on the shoulder St. Germaine said would come as a signal to begin.

It took almost a year before I finally got the go-ahead. I wondered how to proceed. A fun way, I thought, would be to first determine how many of my paintings would be in the book. I did this by using a pendulum and dowsed for an answer. (Dowsing was originally a type of divination using a y-shaped twig or a metal rod to find water or oil.) I was taught by a master dowser to dowse using a pendulum with a semi-precious stone suspended from a chain to ask "yes" and "no" questions. When the stone would swing one direction, it meant "yes" to the question and when it would swing the other direction, the answer was "no."

With this method I found that there were to be eighteen paintings in the book, sixteen of which were completed, leaving me with only two to paint. Next, I dowsed over almost every painting I had, and asked with the pendulum, "Are you to be in Book II?" When I got a "yes," I put those in a "yes" pile. When I counted the "yeses" there were exactly sixteen paintings, and that, for some reason, really astounded me.

"I am being guided," I thought. "This is really going to happen!"

The combined energy of the paintings which had been chosen looked beautiful to me and felt powerful. Not long after, in meditation, I saw the vision for the first painting in the book, *As Above, So Below* (pg. 16), and the book was on its way.

All of the paintings in this book are mandalas, or sacred circles, which I had started painting about ten years earlier, for the peace, balance and healing they brought to my life. They were, and still are for me, an incredibly wonderful format for my personal creative expression as well as a place to center and connect with my inner spirit. It has been said that the nature of God is a circle and that may be explanation enough for why I paint mandalas. I like to be and need to be in that energy. I believe they kept me alive. It is noteworthy to mention that in all the mandalas I painted, including the ones for this book, my intention was to co-create the mandala with spirit, and I always began by first writing that on the back of the painting. Then, as I painted, I knew that both my creation and I were being guided.

After the paintings were chosen, how they were to be arranged and when and how the writing was to be done, was still a mystery. I trusted that I would know what to do when the time came. I began to happen upon old writings from my guides which I'd forgotten I had, and noticed how perfectly they explained some of the paintings. It became a treasure hunt. I started to put old messages with new paintings and new messages with old paintings. I seemed to have all the information I needed, already. I moved everything around like musical chairs until I finally began to get a sense of the overall direction the book was going. I was then able to divide the book into four sections where the messages and the paintings seemed to fit into a kind of progression from beginning, to middle, to the end, and back again. It was like a giant mandala, one in which the whole idea was always present, although unseen, and only understood when it was completed.

Once I had the four sections, the format of the book seemed clear. Within each section and pertaining to it, I included messages I received from different guides and teachers from the past to the present. Each message is preceded by a short explanation about the circumstances in which I came to receive the information. Mandala paintings of either flowers or colors illustrate many of the messages. Finally, I included a short narrative about each painting—and there was always a story behind every mandala I painted. At times there was something about the watercolor technique I used, the format I chose or the effect the color or the painting had on me. Whatever I found to be interesting I added, and whether or not I said it every time, each painting was healing for me in some way.

The messages span the time from the beginning of my receiving guidance to the present. They are offered for other's to use "as is," or as an inspiration to request and receive guidance from one's own teachers, guides or inner self.

This book started with a simple urging of inner guidance. From the start, I felt I was being cradled, protected and deeply loved by all of my guides. And, as the book grew, just holding it energized me. That kept me going. I learned things about color, light and flowers, and I grew spiritually and healed outside the accepted norms of reality. And, what and how I learned, I believe couldn't have been learned in any other way. It was a journey that lasted longer than I had originally expected. When I first thought the book was complete I put it on the shelf and waited for further guidance. And, I thought I was complete as well. But I wasn't. I had more healing to do and that came with a journey through breast cancer. It hit me hard and I definitely went through a dark time. Everything I thought I knew seemed to be ripped out from under me and I felt lost and empty for a while. When I finally began to paint again, I created an enormous amount of mandalas, grabbing on to them as a way to pull myself out of the dark hole I appeared to be in. Years later, I finally realized some of those paintings needed to be added to this book. I first had to warm up to that idea. Those mandalas carried such a charge and touched such a tender place inside me, I had to be ready. When those paintings were added, with explanations of the circumstances in which they were painted, it provided another part of my story to share—of growth: emotionally, spiritually and artistically. Now I see that this book wouldn't have been complete without them. The writing about those paintings is mostly from me, punctuated with an occasional message from my guides. It became apparent that the reason the book took so long to come together was because I needed time to really grasp the full meaning of what my guides said would be a "shift." Perhaps I was being tempered, but I was definitely being healed.

And so, I present to you the adventure, just as it happened.

As St. Francis told me:

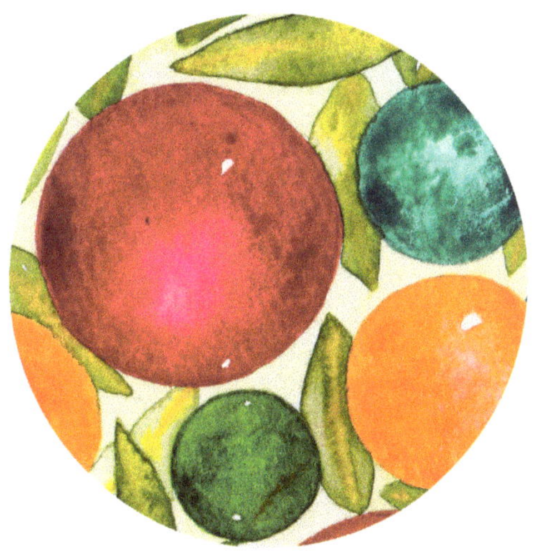

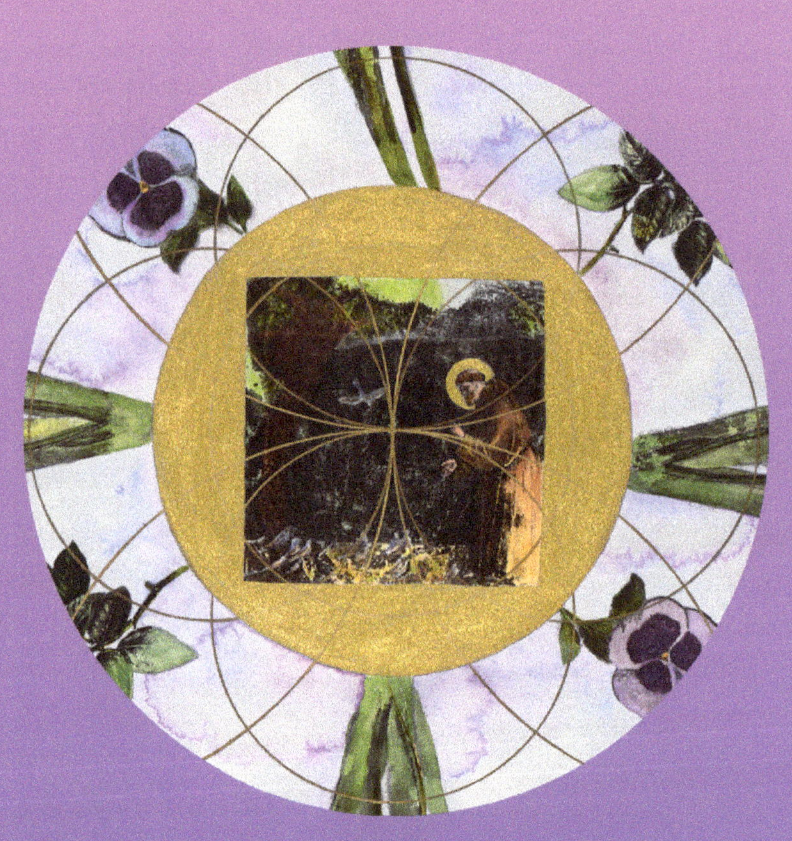

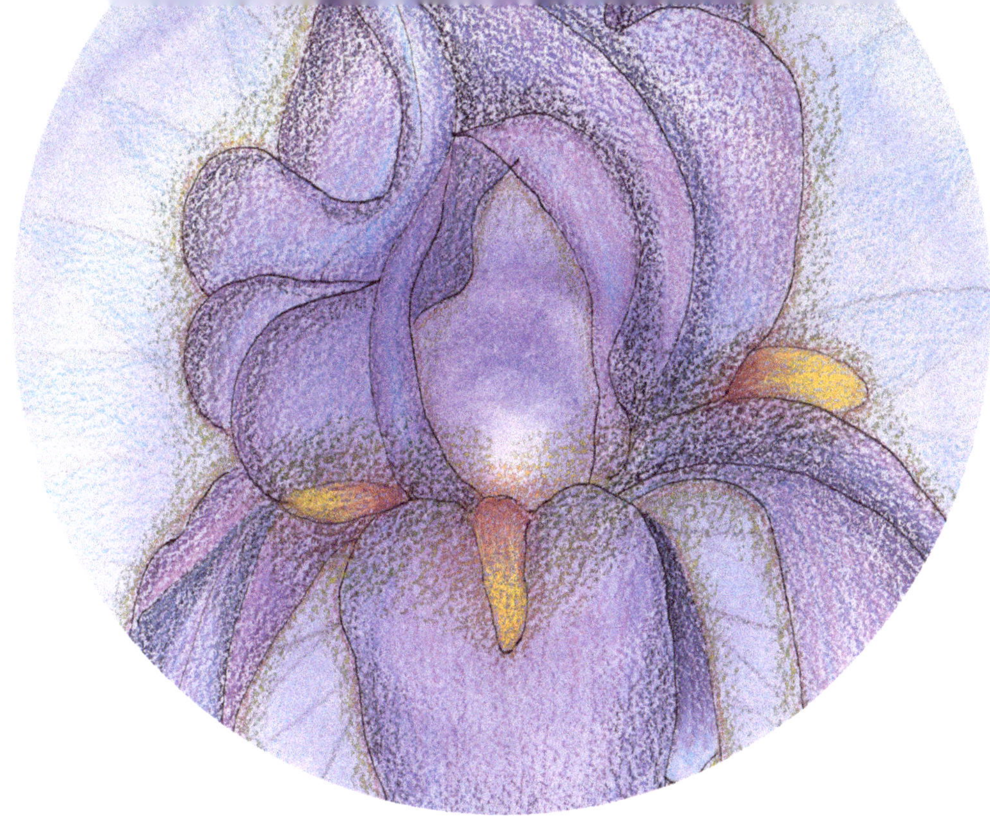

PART I

THE BEGINNINGS OF A NEW VENTURE

Part I is about beginnings and awakenings and contains some of the initial written messages I received from St. Germaine and St. Francis about the book and its purpose. St. Francis is my other main guide for the book. It is here where the announcement came that there would be a new book "we would write together," and the purpose of the book would be a purification for me as I shared the power of light and color with others. The essence of the material has remained the same through the years. From the onset I was told to paint, be with my flowers, use color to bring the love of God alive in myself and others, and that color was "the key to know God and to heal." From this would come a "new life" and an "awakening" and the messages, illustrated with the paintings, show the ways that this was to come about. It was here, at the beginning, that St. Francis said to me:

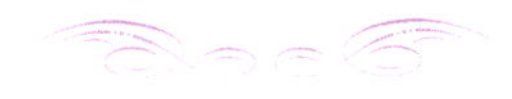

A NEW VENTURE
A MESSAGE FROM ST. FRANCIS
APRIL 29, 1987

This was the first written message I ever received from St. Francis. It came following his initial appearance in 1987, (more on that in "Opening to Indigo," pg. 34). Needless to say, that was a profound experience, one which changed my life. His words were simple, direct and reassuring and have remained consistent through the years.

We are here with you again. The time is right. The place is right. The setting is right. We are here in support of you and your

— 11 —

spiritual pursuits. We support you. We will work with you every day. Now begin. Ask for guidance. But know we are always near. This is a new venture. We are right here with you. We are helping you. Tune in. Paint. Be with your flowers as much as possible. This will make the shift solid—secured. Yes, what you felt today was true. You can work from your center, and make money, or energy, flow toward you. As you are flowing in harmony—harmony will flow toward you. We can't stress this enough—to be in your yard with your flowers. This will solidify your shift and make you very aware of us—attached, connected. In order for you to make your way you need to be connected to us and stay connected. We will work together in creating your new life. You have wanted this for a long time. We open our arms as you accept us, let us in and hear us. We are pleased to work with you. For you to open to the light fully. Good, the time is now. Your shift has begun. Now we will make it bigger and bigger—degree by degree; step by step. Just like anything you do with accomplishment in mind. One step at a time. We will work together toward making you the success you already are. You will grow into it. We have enjoyed talking with you and send you joy.

Your Counselors and

St. Francis

Use Color
A Message From Vincent Van Gogh
March 16, 1988

This message was my first about color, the use of it and my connection to color. It started first as an awareness of yellow completely surrounding me. Everywhere I looked I saw yellow, which actually became a little eerie. And then I could not only sense Van Gogh's presence, but could see his face and orange beard in my mind's eye. His message has taken me years to fully take in.

Immerse yourself in color to feel the splendor of the fullest life has to give. The fullest joy. In color you can feel such exquisite joy, and know life deeply and intensely. Use color to the extreme—more than you ever have or ever considered doing. Color is life being fully lived. Color is joy. Color is God. Bathe in it. Use it. Be sensitive to it for it truly is "God Manifest" as you observed in one of your paintings. There is much more to color than people really know. It can be used for healing for it is truly God's light stepped down so it can be seen by you. Color is the smile of God that you can see. It is life in its fullest beauty and truth. It is love in its fullest most expansive sense, expanding and uncontainable, boundary-less. It is truly the fullest sense of joy—for joy is overflowing, ever-expanding, uncontainable and unlimited.

Think about it. Think about the colors. Bright, beautiful, powerful, joyful red; warm, intense and joyous orange; happy, laughing, alive and smiling yellow; caring, growing, loving and grounded green; free, beautiful and serene blue; blissful, intense, romantic and lovely indigo; and royal, powerful, bright and exciting violet. You see, do you know of anything more beautiful than color—for all things that are beautiful are color.

Teach color. Teach others to love color. To love their intensity, their brightness, their light, love and full measure of joy. Open others up to color—to appreciate color, to understand color, to bring color into their lives. Color will heal them and attune them to the truth that is God, to that joy that is God. For when you are attuned to the vibrations of color you are truly connected to the power that is God, to the joy that is God.

To the power that is within—to the God that is within. Color will release that joy and connect you with God.

You see, you are smiling—for you know of what I speak, because you are able to experience these sensations and make your connection with God. You long for the experience of this connection and you bask in it with glory when you feel it.

This is the greatest feeling you can ever have—basking in the light of God, and we commend you for this desire that you yearn for so. But you know how to make this connection, and now, in your classes we suggest to help others do the same. The students will not at first understand or know what you are doing, but each will come to know in their own way and own time. Ask for guidance on how you may reach them for only the Father knows how to do this. There is great value in this work that you will be doing. It is the greatest value. You must understand this and accept it. You are giving the greatest gift which you must understand before others will understand. The Father values this and therefore you simply cannot not value this joy you are sharing with others.

I did not do this in my lifetime. I did not value myself, who I was, what I did—the essence of me. And because of this, I was not valued by others. I took my value then, in turn, from the outside and not from within where I did feel the love of God. I wanted to express this and did not know how, and in what I did, the intensity of this that I tried to get across, made me seem crazy. I did not value my connection that I had with God so that I could have had peace. No. I fought it and found no peace. I searched and searched for a way to express my love of God, my joy, the intense feeling I felt of ecstasy in my connection with God, but my powerful emotions of trying to prove myself got in the way. This is what people

saw. This is what they remembered. They did not know what I was trying to say. They were not ready. I am known not as I really was, which was a man who so loved God and wanted to share that love.

We can work together now in bringing that love of God alive inside others. Color is the key. Opening their eyes to color will open their hearts to God.

Call on me anytime so that we may work together with love in our hearts and the expectancy of joy in the hearts of others.

I am yours in service,

Vincent

We Are Going To Write A Book Together
A Message From St. Germaine
January 6, 2000

Just days into the new millennium I sensed St. Germaine was near and had a message. I was also feeling a desire to go deeper within myself. And so, on my morning walk, I got the words clearly, "We are going to write a book together." This was the first I knew of this book. I had been working on a book about mandalas with St. Germaine's help and wondered if that was what he was referring to, or was this a new project and the first one would be abandoned. That did give me a bit of a sinking feeling. When I got home, I asked, "St. Germaine, What is your message to me?"

My dear, fear not, for whatever is good and right for you will happen as it should and in the proper timing. This is what you should be focusing on—what is your true work and how can you open up to it so that it flows easily through you. This should be your focus now.

And, you must stay connected to your deeper wells within you, trusting now even more, that you are doing as you should and as you chose to and agreed to upon entering here. You have a very precious part to play in this ensuing drama of earth's unfolding. It is most beautiful and most needed. Your light and your color will help many and when you are on that wavelength you are doing well your chosen work. It is a most honored and most high task that you have chosen and been chosen to. We honor you and you must know we are always with you, as we have told you many times before. The time has come now where you will enter fully into your right work. We know you feel at times that it has taken overlong to reach this place. But, we say to you, you have been in training and preparation, for the strength it will take to do this wonderful and much needed work. Stay pure, stay always connected and your channel will remain always as it should be—connected to the One. Be happy for this great work you will be doing and the light you will be sharing with others.

As to your first book, fear not, all is well. But there is a very, very special book coming that you and I will be doing together. Know this and be ready for the tap on the shoulder when it comes. You will be shown what to do. The writing in it will come as this is—with purity and from Spirit. Be open and ready. Love God always and it will flow to you easily and with no hesitations. It will not be hard for you, but rather a joy and another spiritual practice which we know you so diligently pursue. It is another way of purification for you and we honor your desire to participate on the flow of God's Love.

And, yes, as you have guessed, it will be about color, and the power that is in color that so many, and even yourself, do not yet fully comprehend. It will be most beautiful.

Stay open to this beauty, color and light and notice what effect these have on you. This is how you'll start—as you are now, by balancing your chakra system daily. You are already noticing the difference in how you feel. Pay heed to these changes—for they are mighty. And, strong will you become, by and through light and color.

And, yes, you can start by continuing on the track you were on this morning. Noticing the flowers, their shape and design, the rich colors, their intricate centers and using them as a way to focus and bring through their color and energy. These will make exquisite Flower Energy Paintings. And they will bring through, hold and diffuse the energy for those who gaze upon them. They will have the ability to heal for they will carry the Love of God.

This is your mission—and it is truly bringing spirit into matter as you chose. It is a great mission and we honor you highly. Stay focused on God, stay in the light and all will be well. And, you will be richly rewarded on many levels, including within your monetary system, the one in which you are overly concerned with now. But, that worry will one day fade as you become fully and deeply and completely enveloped in this your love work.

Bless you, in deepest love and respect,
St. Germaine and Friends on the ray

Let Color Into Your Heart

A Message from St. Francis
January 22, 2001

After receiving the previous message, I wondered, "Is it time to get started on the book with St. Germaine?" The next message told me the book was on its way. It took a year, and more preparation than I expected. I also learned there were others involved in the project.

You are connected to the Universe. Yes, you have heard correctly—and seen correctly. We are with you as we have always told you we are. And, now you are feeling us, and understanding more. Congratulations. This is a wonderful event in your growth toward and in spirit. You are awakening. You have in fact seen correctly the vision we have presented of the big tree with lights, and realized, also correctly, it was like a human form—aglow in light and energy. You saw as well its reflection of itself in the earth, marveling at this image, and not quite understanding it. We are here to explain—and to help as we are asked, in the reproduction of this scene and its essence in your colorful medium, watercolor.

This tree and its mirror reflection is like the human body and its energy systems, or centers. As above, so below, as you have heard before. You have been noticing in your own energy system lately, how the colors are flowing, how the energies are moving, and the places in yourself where they are not. This is as it should be. We are showing you how it all works. You have been feeling what you would call a "burning" and have sensed that there is a clearing going on in your energy which causes an increase in your energy's frequency. Thank you for being aware, for paying attention. You have also felt that with this increase in frequency that you are more connected to the cosmos—and this is correct as well. When you clear your body, your vehicle, this allows for a higher vibration to flow in your energy system. With a clearer and higher vibration it allows you to connect and flow with the energy of the universe—in harmony and in unity. Congratulations for this intention, even though you may not have been totally and consciously aware that you were going there or even how to get there. But, there is really here, and you are in the now and in the flow.

And you have, on some level, wanted this for a long time.

One of the things that opened you up to this was your use of the transmuting Violet Flame of St. Germaine (see "Using the Violet Transmuting Flame," pg. 71). The heavens sang when you began in earnest to use his help, his decrees. Again, congratulations.

So you were given, prior to your experience of it, a vision of how to clear your energy through work with color and light. From your message on clearing blockages, which you just rediscovered today (see "Clearing Your Energy Centers," pg. 60) you see that it is important to ground this work in the earth. The earth is here to help you, and all. And to quote one of your Native American wise men, "The earth is one of your greatest spiritual teachers."

Involve the Earth in your self-healing, in your clearing and always honor it, its four directions and give thanks for what it continues to provide you. When you heal your earth body, through the work with the colors which is one of your greatest gifts, then you will heal your spirit body. And when you heal your spirit body, you may enter into the realm of the divine cosmos and flow with all love, all harmony, all unity. This will open you to such joy you have never known, and this is where the real adventures begin.

Keep smiling, and stay tuned,

yours in loving kindness and service,

your guide and teacher

St. Francis and all

You have long wanted an answer to your questioning of what color is and does. The answer has been given you in your experience of opening your heart to color. My message to you and all: Slow down, open up and let color into your heart. It is everywhere around you. Let it in to awaken you.

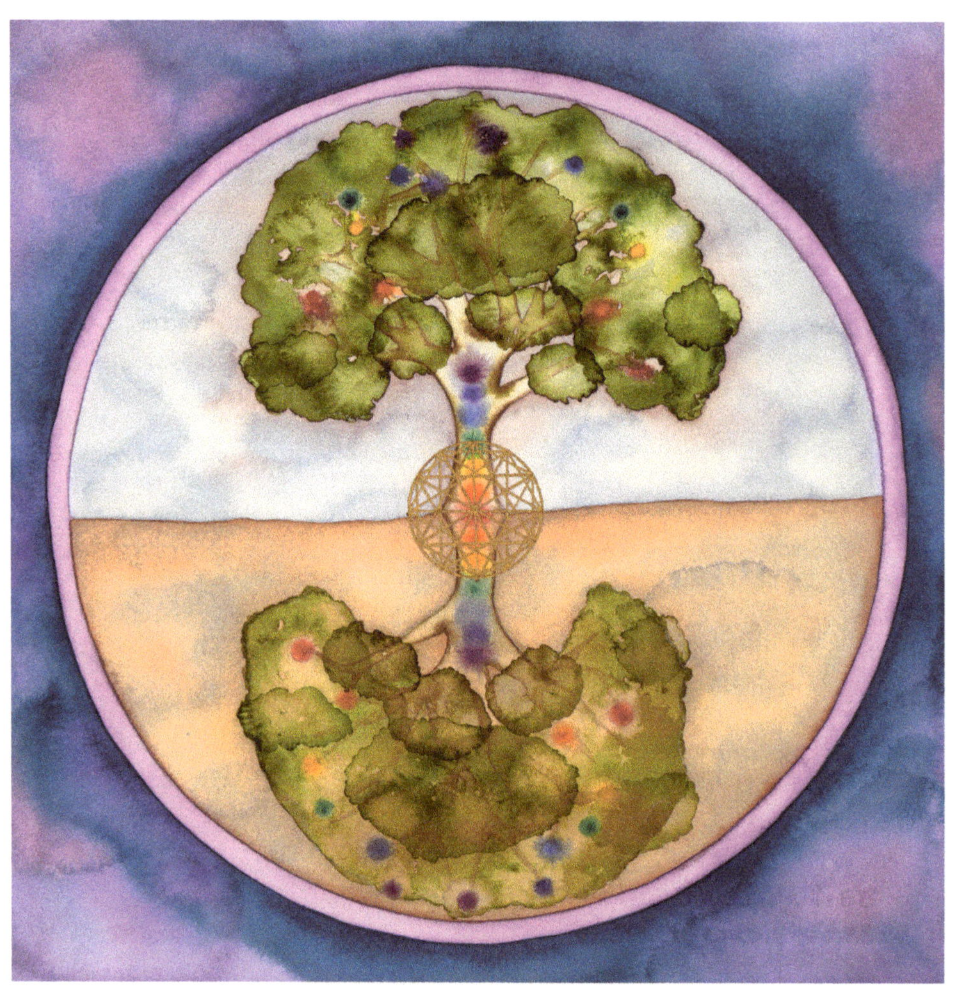

"As Above So Below"

Watercolor, gold ink, 15" x 15" 2001

This is the image I saw in meditation, referred to in St. Francis' message, of a tree full of colored lights and its reflected image in the earth. My mind, initially trying to make sense of it, thought it was an inspiration for our next Christmas card! Before I attempted the painting, I was glad to have happened upon a forgotten message I had received in 1987. It said: We are pleased you have made direct contact. You can do this. The heavens sing as you join us. The picture in your mind of the heavens and the earth with the oak tree connecting them is a beautiful one and a good symbol of the reality. You may want to paint this someday. Should you do this, ask for our assistance and we will be there. I was told this message came from "God, the Heavenly Angels and the Nature Spirits," the first and only time I'd received a message from a group such as these. I was amazed at the connection so many years later, and, of course, did ask for help.

LOVE AND THE LIGHT BODY
MESSAGES FROM MY GUIDES
AND HIGH SELF
JUNE 6, 2000

My guides were telling me that in awakening to color, we awaken our heart and open to love. Through two similar messages I received one week, I was being asked to move forward in love and into my highest self. I've combined the two here with an earlier painting *Show Your Colors* on the next page.

Dear One,

You have gotten the message—and it is about Love. It is the lesson you are learning and will continue to learn until you become steeped in it. Love is all there is! Go out into the world and carry love. Ignite all you meet with love and in so doing deepen your own love within your heart. This will heal all things and cure all things.

When you work, work with love and within love. Make your work about love, for love, because of love. Let it be your guiding light and golden torch.

Make it the reason you do all things. All things will bear your glow. The ultimate lesson— and you are not far from it—Life full of love. Love creates all things, expands all things and opens all doors. Which one will you choose to open now? Make it fun—isn't that what you want? Make it full of love, isn't that also what you want? Go for it. Ride the wave. Step into your power. Do not play down any longer who you are, who we are. You are now moving into your Goddess-self. Stand tall and do not be less than you are. In standing tall, and accepting who you are, you will be all you can be and have all that you want and need. Just ask—ask from the highest you— for you deserve and should have it all, all the best. For you are the best, fully stepping into the Light Body that you came to be—the light body that we are. This is an exciting time. Stand tall in the presence of the almighty which is within you. You are made New.

Step into me
for I am you and we are one.
From all your guides who love you
more than you know

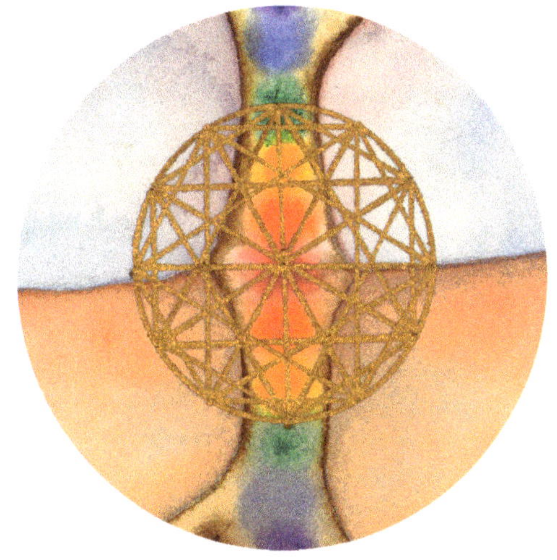

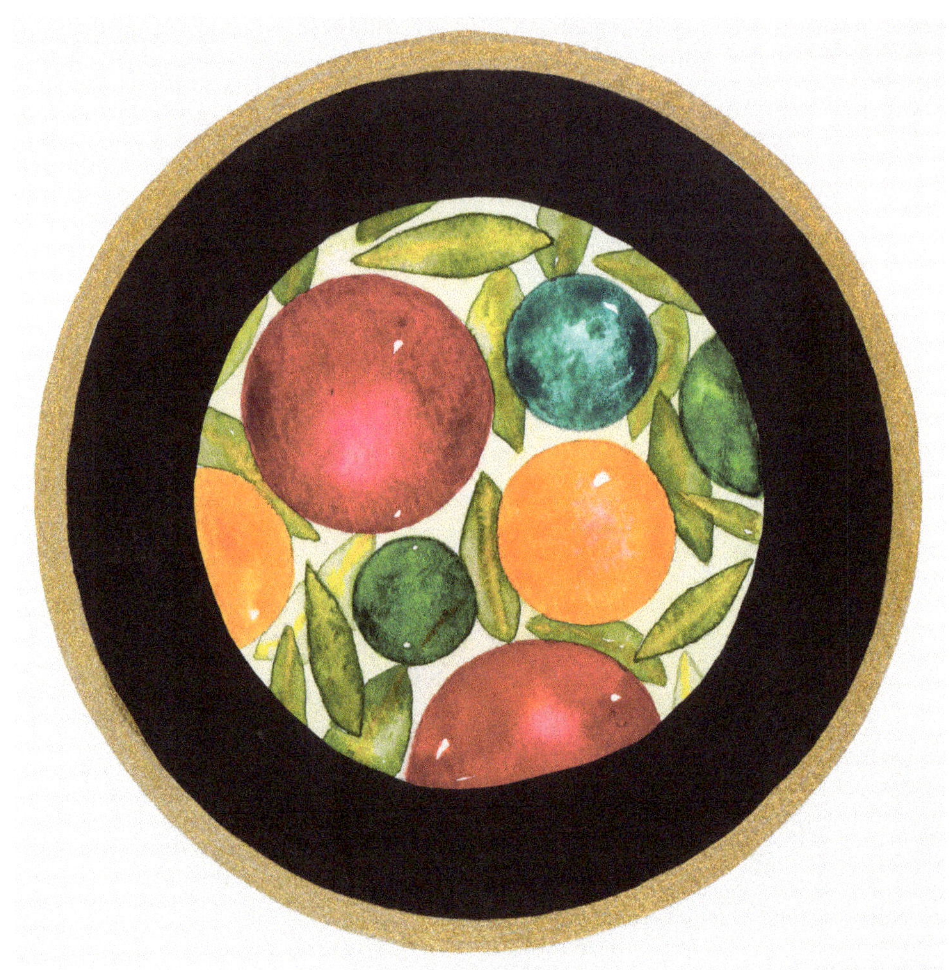

"Show Your Colors"

Watercolor, gold ink, "11 x 11" 1997

Showing your colors means showing your true self. Prior to beginning this painting I had asked, "What color am I today?" This is a representation of what I saw, and "show your colors" I felt was clearly the message. I have come to see this painting as a detail of the previous tree with lights—a close-up of the color, light and energy with which any of us can be aglow. It shows the colors and light that I was that particular day, in the winter during the holiday season. Everyday our light shines, and I believe we are being told here not to hold it back. What colors are you today? Show your colors and the light that you truly are.

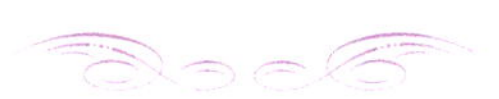

The Beginning Of A New Way, A New Life

Here is information from a female messenger about the necessity of connecting with feminine energy to open the heart.

Thank you for acknowledging me and opening up a path of communication. I am always with you, as you have been told many times over by your other guides and teachers. I am the one you have seen as the head of your group of light workers on the other side and who you endearingly call "the boss." You have wondered who I really am, and I am your high self---the feminine energy of your spiritual self. I am in charge of this group and oversee them and all of your spiritual activities. I am the bridge between your life on earth and the fuller life of your spirit and who you really are. I am in charge now because the feminine energy within you needs to come forward and be balanced with the masculine. Your masculine energy has been dominant within you for a long time and now it must give over to a more balanced way. Your masculine drive, without the balance of the feminine, could have killed you, and your illness (Chronic Fatigue Syndrome) was the beginning of a new way, a new life and it needed to be born out of the feminine energy. Now, you didn't know what that was, who it was or how to do it. This is why I am here and am now in charge. You have wondered of my name, and Grace has come to you, and that is the essence of my work, our work, here. Think about Grace. My work is about the circle of being and not about the linear power of doing. When you see your light workers in your mind's eye, you see us correctly in a strategy room, all in a circle, all around you, loving you, nurturing you and caring for you. We have created a vessel of blessing and you are in our care at its center. We are all so pleased that you can sense us and our work together. It is such a blessing and we all enjoy making your life the blessed event. You are learning to receive well, and that is your job for now. It is important to give and even more so to know how to graciously receive for you are truly receiving God's great love for you. We bring that to you and we commend you on your opening up and receiving it. We are blessed to be able to give to you and in so doing teach you how to receive. This opens your heart, and we know this is what you have longed for. An open heart!

We are so pleased that you have welcomed our communication and acknowledged our work together. We delight in your time with us in your morning meditation when you ask "the boss" what your job is for the day. You always smile at this, and we smile with you. And we are happy to give guidance about your spiritual path. Sometimes we know it is not what you expect, but relaxing and flowing in harmony is still a lesson for you, and not always easy to do for a doer!

We are always with you,
in deep love and respect,
your Grace,
always in service to your Highest Self

You are wondering about your guides whom you have seen as masculine. Actually, all are of balanced energy, not more of one energy than another. You have seen them as masculine because you thought that was where the power was. It was what you were taught, and are now learning a new way. I am like a Divine Mother to you, overseeing the energies around you and directing them for your highest good.

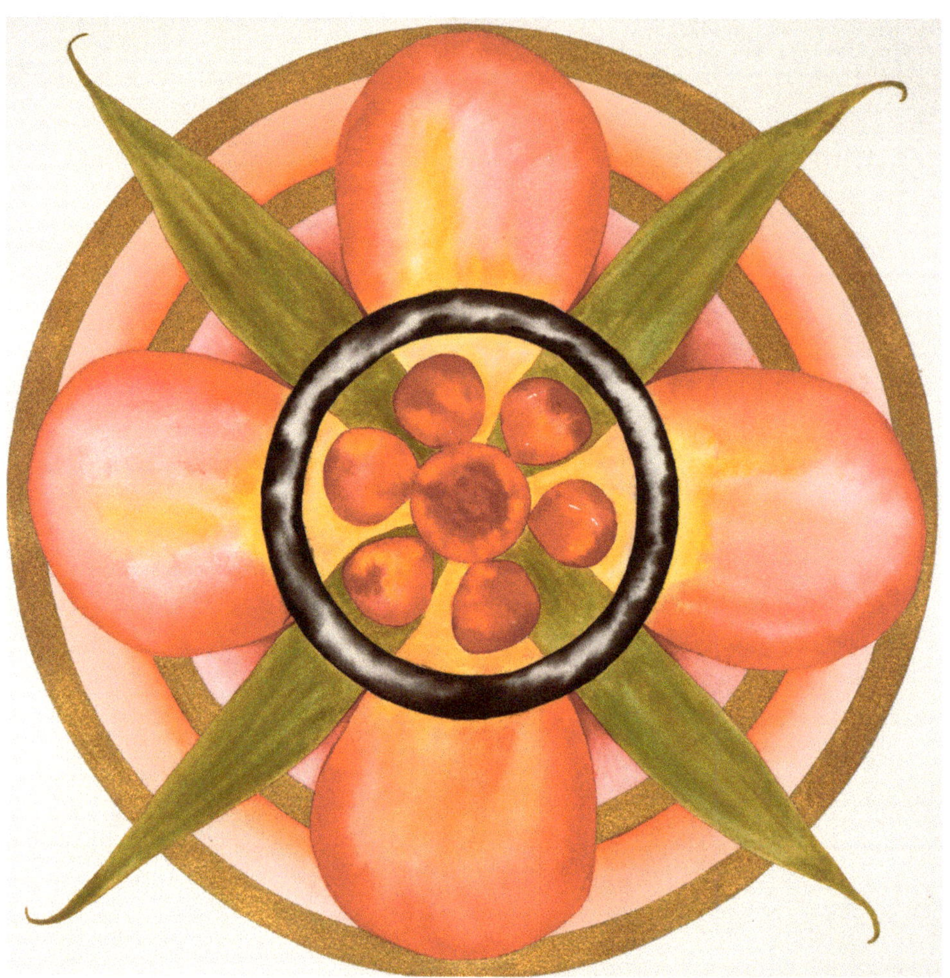

"Shakti"

Watercolor, gold ink, 15" x 15" 1996

The inspiration for this image came with an experience on Thanksgiving week-end, when I participated in a spiritual initiation ceremony in which the *shakti* was awakened within me. *Shakti,* or supreme energy, is whom the sages of India wor-ship as the Mother of the Universe. Believed to be grace bestowing, this initiation is called *shaktipat,* and is the gentle re-awakening of the divine spiritual energy within given by a spiritual teacher from an ancient lineage. In the ceremony I expe-rienced, colors exploded in my heart like the aurora borealis and I had a vision of light pouring onto me through a rose cathedral window. On a short break, I quickly made my way across the street to San Francisco's Grace Cathedral and went to each stained glass window and image of Christ and found myself saying, "I'm back....I AM BACK! I vow to do the work." I felt so much love and deep connection.

Earlier that year I had walked the labyrinth at Grace Cathedral for the first time. This ancient image of sacred geometry is said to invite the Holy Spirit into our lives, the essence of which, according to the Labyrinth Project founder, is the feminine side of God. In the labyrinth experience I felt that my soul work, which on some level I was remembering as very ancient, spiritual and familiar, seemed to call to me and I surrendered and committed myself to it. Now combined with the *shakti* awakening, I felt a deep, wonderful reconnection to my spiritual source. Very shortly after that I began my first book on mandalas. This is a painting of what the *shakti* felt like to me—intense, fiery, and powerful. It was an attempt to understand what had happened to me, and just what the "*shakti*" was.

Your Work
A message From all Your Guides
February 22, 2002

Here is a powerful message about what my guides called my "life's work." But first I had to get myself out of fear and out of my own way.

As for your paintings, and your desire to get back to your work, take one day at a time. Be gentle with yourself. Do not try to do big spiritual paintings when that is not what you feel. Paint what you feel. Love over fear. Overcoming fear. The truth. For the truth will set you free. It is hard to face sometimes—but it must be. Face it gently and lovingly. Paint your connection to the earth and find your truth this way. Let the earth help you. This will help you become grounded. For this is what you need—and as you can see the reaction in your body now— you fear it. The fear coming all the way into your body and you resist. You resist being who you fully are—and who you fully are will be in your body and connected to the earth. Seek from the earth your paintings—for it has much to say and much help for you. Connect, do not be afraid, for it will be a wonderful experience for you— and you are deeply connected to the earth. You have just forgotten and this challenge, remember, is reminding you of your deep connection, not to forget it, acknowledge it and give it a voice. You know things, and have not said. Give them voice, this is what you are here for. All the way to the depths of the earth, from your high tower of spirituality. But there is deep spirituality in the earth, deep loving, caring, knowledge, healing. You can bring this message through— here are your next paintings. Ask the earth what it needs to say and bring it through—say it. You have a deep profound connection to the voice of the earth. Fear—why this is what you have been afraid of—moving from the higher realms to the earth and then through your body which you have blocked. Don't block the energy any longer. Ask and you shall find help.

I am happy you are listening. This is a most profound message and life's work. Begin it now and you shall be healed and the Earth shall be healed. For she will be loved and heard and finally understood.

We bless you and love you beyond measure.
All your guides including Ishtar
and energies from the earth

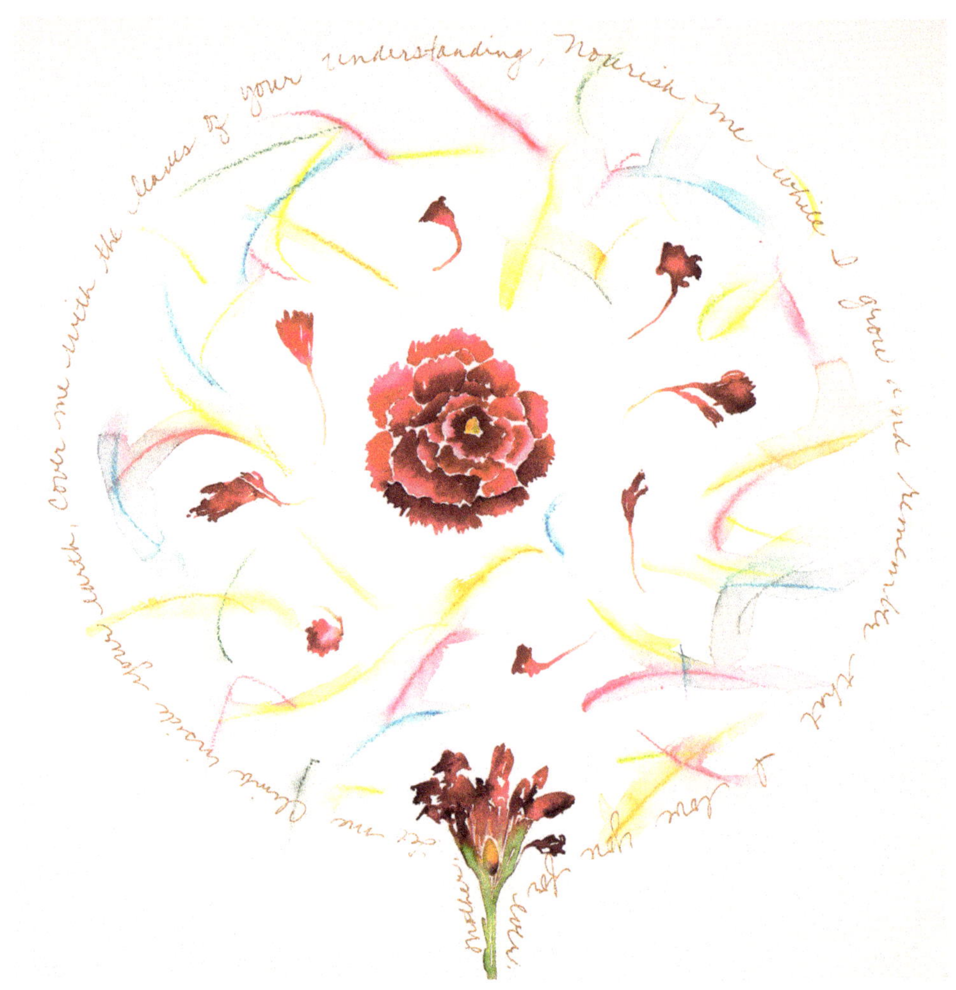

ABOUT THE PAINTING

"Mother, Let Me Climb Inside Your Earth"

Watercolor, watercolor crayons, gold ink, 15" x 15" 1994

Mother,

Let me climb inside your Earth,

Cover me with the leaves of your understanding,

Nourish me while I grow,

And remember

That I love you forever.

One winter I had four colds, one after another. Very curious as to why this was happening, I used the mandala process and painted this painting with the intention of healing. What I quickly realized, as I centered into myself before beginning, was what I really wanted was mothering and nurturing. I touched into sadness and feelings of "never having gotten enough" mothering came to the surface. Red always seemed to be mother to me, and so I began with the red carnation in the center as I acknowledged the feelings of neediness. But as I proceeded, I was amazingly uplifted by feelings of profound nurturing, caring and protection from Mother Earth. Spontaneously I wrote the words around the circle, which just seemed to fit. It was a wonderful experience, and I did heal, not getting a cold again for a long time. I took the carnation apart as I painted it, and told myself it was to look at and understand how to paint each petal. But I think I was really taking the whole mothering thing apart and trying to understand it.

A couple of years later I was sitting next to a man from Milan on a bus traveling to a spiritual center in upstate New York. We struck up a conversation about our journey and soon we were talking about the longing to know God. He told me of something called the "great longing." He said it was a longing in an individual for more love from one's mother, which could be felt as an emptiness which was never completely filled. He said it was that longing which kept us searching and eventually led us back to God. What are we really searching for? Something a human mother can never give us—the return to our source, Mother/Father God.

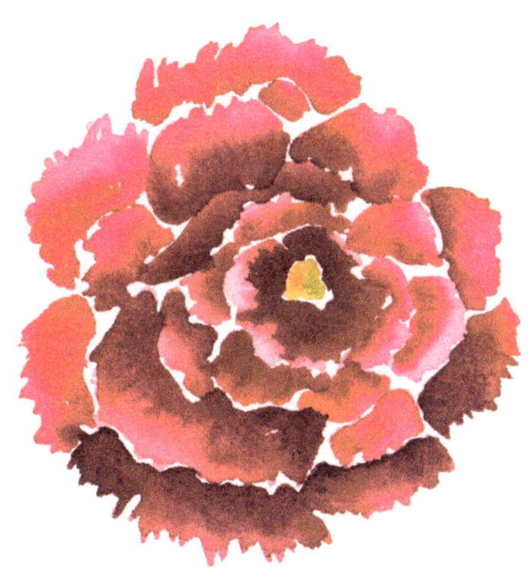

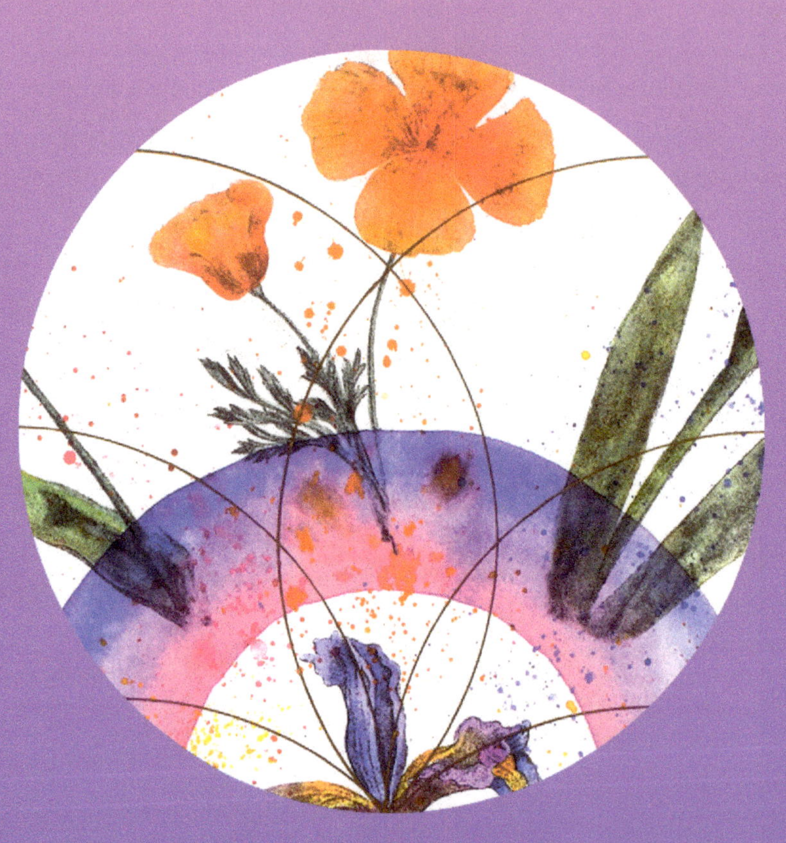

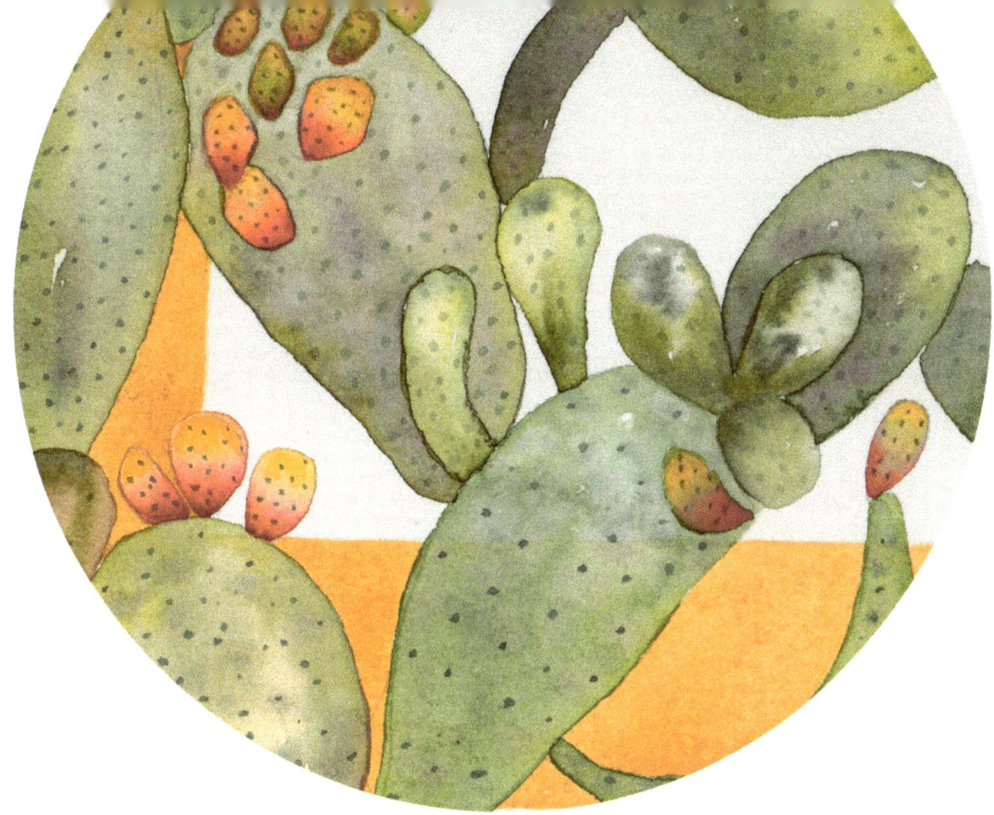

PART II

FLOWER ENERGY PAINTINGS:
THE COLORS AND THEIR MESSAGES

A message I received from St. Germaine quite a while ago told me to "go outside and bathe in the colors of nature. Breathe it in…Bring your writing book. See what color calls to you and write down what it says to you and do what it tells you to do."* So I did as he told me and went out to the ocean bluff and waited. I wondered if it was going to work as St. Germaine suggested. Eventually green caught my eye and spoke to me. I wrote what was said to me in the form of poetry and what a wonderful experience. I wrote all of the color messages in the same way. I was really quite new to writing poetry and was always amazed as it evolved. I would become aware of the color which seemed to be calling to me, usually a flower, and would sit down as close as I could get to it with my pen and journal. I would breathe in the color, which usually left me feeling "intoxicated" and heady, and

then would write down the message that came. Sometimes the poems are in the form of a dialogue between me and the color, with my words written in regular type and the message from the color in colored type.

There are nine flower mandala paintings, starting with a white calla lily, a red-violet pansy and the spectrum of flowers is completed with violet, indigo, blue, green, yellow, orange and red. Each is followed by a color poem. As for the flower mandalas, when I finally realized in my life that I wanted to make art rather than talk about it (as I did as an art history instructor,) flowers were my first subject of choice. I saw flowers as an expression of spirit, and when I painted them, I asked to channel that spirit through me and into the paintings. I tended to paint flowers in a series, one of each color in the spectrum—it was a way to teach myself about color, about the flowers and how to paint them. I saw the colors in the series of flowers I painted as the chakras, or energy centers in the body. In Eastern art the chakras are represented as flowers in various stages of unfoldment. Starting with red, which is called the root chakra and is located at the base of the spine, the energy centers move up through the center of the body to the crown chakra at the top of the head, which is violet or sometimes white. Once I received the inspiration to paint the "Flower Energy Paintings," the first flower and color I was drawn to was the white calla lily.

The final painting in Part II, page 44, *The Rose in My Heart,* illustrates the power of red. This painting and color turned out to be the most challenging of them all, and it surprised me because I love red. In retrospect, as a subject, red was probably about a one-year process. Red worked on my heart, on my body and every other part of me. It was very intense and that was unexpected. Many physical maladies surfaced during my work with red, yet the color red brought a healing and an opening of my heart that was profound. I also believe red worked on the promise of purification the book would bring me, if I worked with its messages.

All the paintings in the book are mandalas, and all in this section have some form of sacred geometry in them, which was an interesting coincidence, and not really planned. Sacred geometry is the study of geometry and proportion, as the hidden law of nature, embodied in the archetypal forms of the circle, square and triangle. It is a belief that everything in nature is in relationship or proportionate to everything else. I became interested in sacred geometry when I began to see these forms in the visions of my mandalas. I started to include the forms in the mandalas before I knew what they were, primarily to be true to the visions. But it seemed the more of the sacred geometry patterns I painted, the more I saw, and they just felt right to me. It may be that sacred geometry is a way of explaining that everything is related and connected. I have read that sacred geometry is a place where "science and spirit can finally meet."

*You can read the entirety of that message in "Heal Yourself With Color" in Part IV, Tools For Opening Your Heart, page 75.

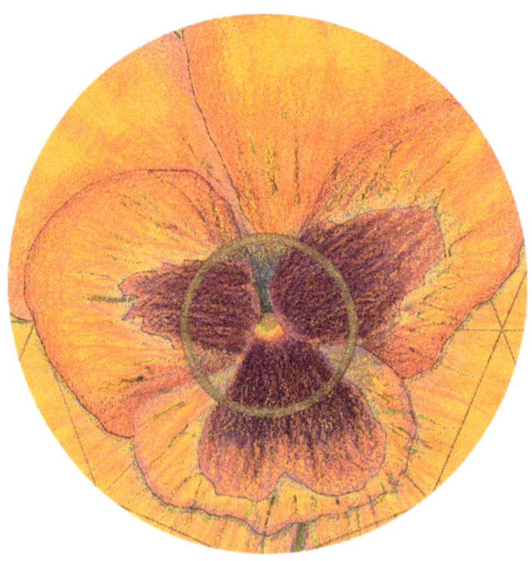

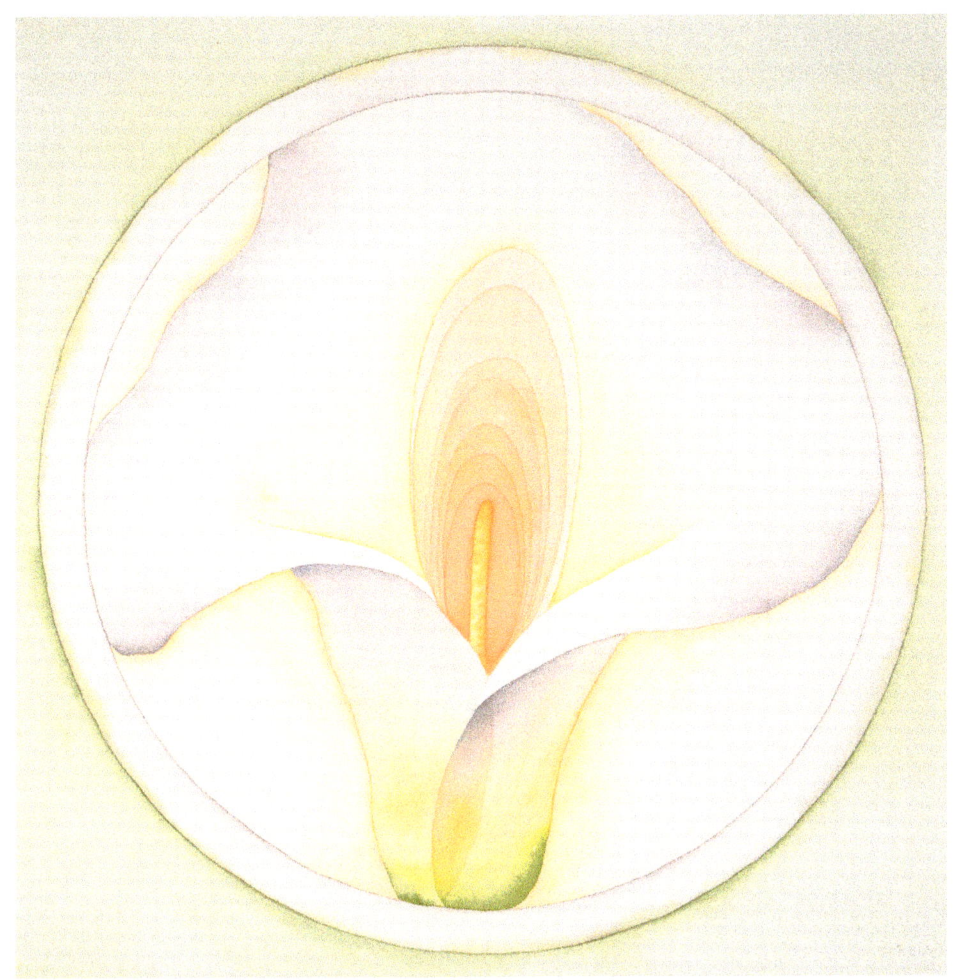

"White: In The Arms Of The All"

Watercolor, 15" x 15" 2000

My heart had been aching as if a flame of love were in it, and it felt really quite wonderful. When I saw the beautiful white calla lily, I perceived a similar flame within it. Now, how to capture that? Painting a white flower is an interesting challenge because in watercolor it means not painting—but letting the white of the paper show through. White areas in watercolor paintings are from the paper and not white paint. As I painted I felt myself letting go and going into the white and being enveloped in a force, an energy I could feel but couldn't see with my normal vision. Being with white, which is all color and no color, and breathing it in from the reflected light in the garden, was profound. It amazed me in its power. No words can really describe it. In the silence, is the All That Is.

After the suggestion from St. Germaine to do "Flower Energy Paintings," and the strong attraction to this calla lily, I heard and responded to the poem and then painted this flower. The whole concept, of color speaking to me and painting the representation of that message, was new, exciting and pushed me to a new level of communication. I was very moved by the experience, and truly felt connected to the All That Is, as I got the message and painted the painting. I originally placed this painting as the last color in the series, thinking I was to start with red, the first chakra, and move to white. As it turned out, I started with white and finished with red.

WHITE: IN THE ARMS OF THE ALL

Flame of my heart
light of my life
surround me and blanket
me in your pure white beauty.
Keep me and hold me within your arms
for I am always in your care.
This beauty, this purity,
what are you my white?
I am all things,
the beginning and the end.
I am the light
which creates all things
and is all things.
Take me into your soul
and know who
I Am.
I am the All That Is.
I am the All That Was.
I am the All That Will Be.
And in me you shall find all things.

In me is all peace, all love
all color and
All That Is.
From within me all things begin
and from within me
all things are cherished
and protected
in the White Fire.

And what is the White Fire?
My love made manifest,
my love made real,
my love made whole and perfect.
I am the All That Is,
whole and free,
and willing to go forth in love
and create all things
from it.
In purity I rest,
in love I manifest
for I am around
and in
and through all.
And, yes, I blanket you,
flame in the heart,
I protect you
and love you
and hold you
always in the purest, perfect love,
touching you in softness
holding you up for
total magnificence—
for you are magnificent
and beautiful
and loved
and surrounded
in the totality of
the beautiful
and pure
White Light.
I am the Light of the World.

Let me feel you
ever so deeply
My Light of the World
and let me carry
within me
within my heart
your magnificence
in the flame of my heart.
And let me carry
this torch
illuminating all
with your light.
And let me become
this light
that I may become
a Legion of Light
for all the world to know you.

Thank you for your grace,
for your love
and for creating me
that I may become
the ultimate in you.
White, white, white,
light of my life,
jewel of my soul
the color from
the flames
dancing in my heart.
Let me know white
Let me know light.
In white I am bathed
and calmed
for I am in your arms,
the Arms of the All.

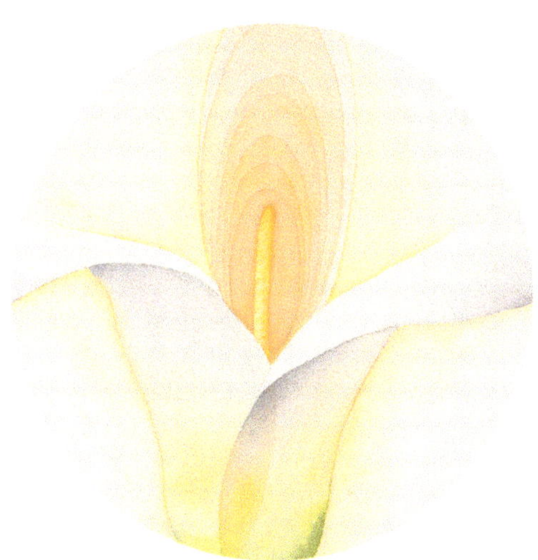

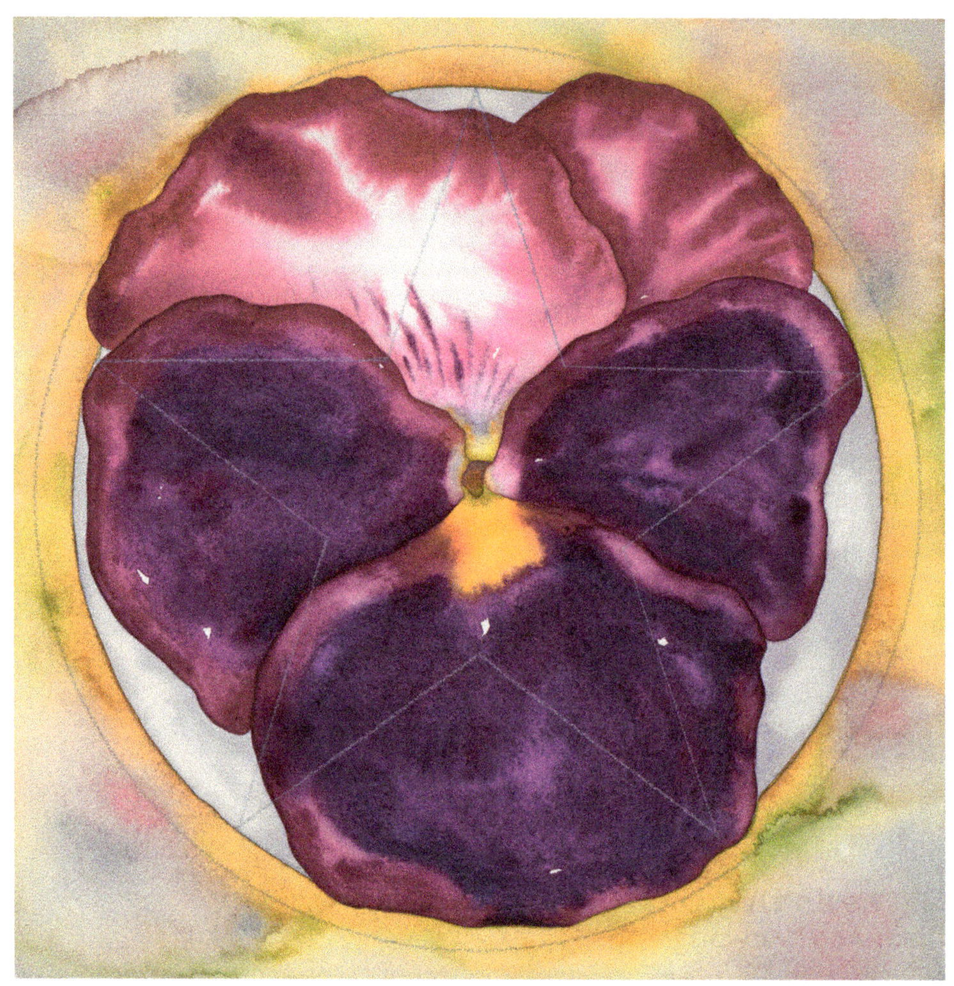

"Red-Violet: The Grace Of Love"

Watercolor, gold ink, "11 x 11" 1997

The color of this friendly pansy electrified me when I saw it in my flower garden. Curiously, it caught my attention and took my breath away; I loved that. The other flowers were very beautiful too, but not as glowing and magical as this one appeared to be that particular day. Painting it was magical as well. It was like being dipped in its exquisite nectar, and I worked diligently to get the color just right. As the work unfolded I let go as much as I could—without dropping the brush and having it roll across the paper! This was truly an experience of co-creation, and I loved that, too. As I completed it, the pansy seemed to call for the five-point star over its five petals. I carefully divided the circle into five equal segments and connected the divisions with a colored pencil to create the ethereal star. White Eagle, one of my spiritual teachers, says that the five-point star is a symbol for the awakening of consciousness, and indicates that the light is beginning to dawn on those who seek it.

Red-Violet:
The Grace Of Love

Jewel in my heart
what have you done to me?
I am weak in the knees
with your cerise, your red-violet.
I am speechless with your beauty
so, speak to me
and tell me what is in your heart
that I may know what illuminates mine.
Your beauty is unspeakable
and makes my heart ache for your love.
Tell me God
who is this that does such a thing to me?
I am at its mercy
and have been brought to my knees.

I am
the joy of God's heart,
the unknowable and unnameable
sweetness of His smile.
I am red-violet,
the color of deep, deep joy,
of such aliveness and such bliss
that the depth is unfathomable.
Open your heart and let me in,
let me in to dwell deep within you
and reach depths
that you know not of.
Let me create such pathways
of love and beauty, of joy and bliss
that you are taken away
from your old self
and find the door to your
new home.
New home, you say.
What of that?
It is a place of such beauty and joy

that your heart skips a beat
and your breath is taken away.
For you are now in the realm of God,
of the All That Is
and your heart has skipped a beat
because you are now in the
Heart of the All
and breathless with ecstasy.
Can you, will you survive?
But, of course,
for that heart is in you and you in it
and we are all together now,
two hearts, beating as one
in the beauty, in the joy
in the ecstasy, and, as always, in the love.
And, this, my dear is your home,
within the heart of unfathomable love.
And, together
we shall go forward
as one.

And, so,
in red-violet,
I am one with the All.
Never apart, never separate,
I know who I am.
I am joy, I am beauty, I am love
And never separate from that
that I am.
I go forward alive
in the heart of God
and God alive in me.
I am blessed, I am loved, I am love
joyfully, happily and gratefully.
In red-violet
I am most blessed
for you have given me a gratitude
I have never known.
I live in the Grace of Love.
And, now I truly know life.

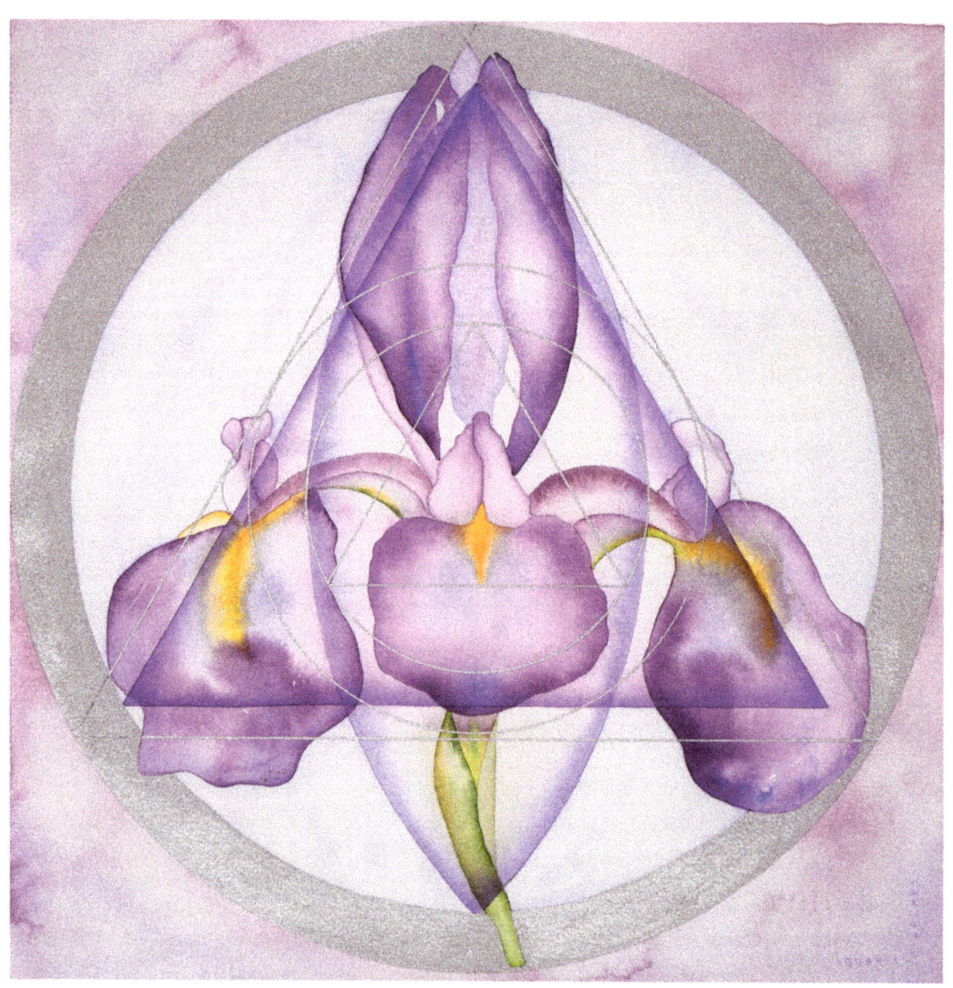

ABOUT THE PAINTING

"IRIS AND TRIANGLE"

Watercolor, silver ink, 15" x 15" 2000

With a triangle gently superimposed over it, this butterfly iris appeared to me one day in meditation. It gave me the impression it was from another dimension. The petals seemed to be reaching to the heavens like hands together in prayer and blessing. There is no flower I've painted more often than the iris. I've always had such a strong attraction to it, even before I knew that the iris, for me, was a symbol of St. Francis. (More of that story in About the Painting, *Opening to Indigo*, pg. 34.) I have since discovered that the iris in Flower Essence Therapy is used for inspiration to "create and to cultivate beauty."* That was such a confirmation to me that I was on the right track, was being guided, and had been for a long time.

*Patricia Kaminski & Richard Katz, *Flower Essence Repertory,* pg. 151, 1992.

— 32 —

VIOLET: AT HOME
WITHIN MYSELF

Violet, violet, violet,
reveal your mystery to me,
take me to your leader!
Who are you and what knowledge
have you for me?
My heart is open and I breathe you in.
Surround me with your beauty
and touch my heart divinely.

I am here for you and all of Earth
and bring you peace, energy and divine glory.
I am violet
the color of love and divine forgiveness.
I am the color of
letting go and being free
to flow with such a grand glory
that your heart opens
to flow with the All That Is.
And what kind of freedom is this, you ask?
It is the freedom of release,
release of your small self,
your limited self,
to the truth of who you are.
The truth will set you free.
Can you breathe it in?
Can you allow that possibility?
Can you flow with God,
with all of creativity,
opening, growing, uplifting
yourself from the bondage
you have created
and believed in overlong?
With violet you can know
that the spark of God is within you.
Violet lets you know the truth.
You are a spark of God

and in living it,
opening and trusting it,
you will be set free.
The violet will do that!
Yes, set you free.
Breathe in the violet,
and you shall see.
It wants to take you, can't you feel it?
Where is it taking you? Inside yourself
to meet yourself
maybe for the first time?
Hello. It's you?
The spark of God who is me?
How could this be?
Just try it, go there and see.
I am you. I am violet
who takes you to yourself
and sets you free.

And, so in violet I am free,
I have touched the divine---
I am divine, and, in being me,
I am free.
What freedom is this?
The only true freedom,
for I am at one
with God. I am at home
within myself.
What a place to find—
I guess this is what they call
Heaven.
Oh, it's such a peaceful place,
I feel so free.
I could stay here forever.
This is Heaven!
Thank you violet.
You have been so attractive
and yet so illusive,
patiently waiting for me to recognize
who I really am.

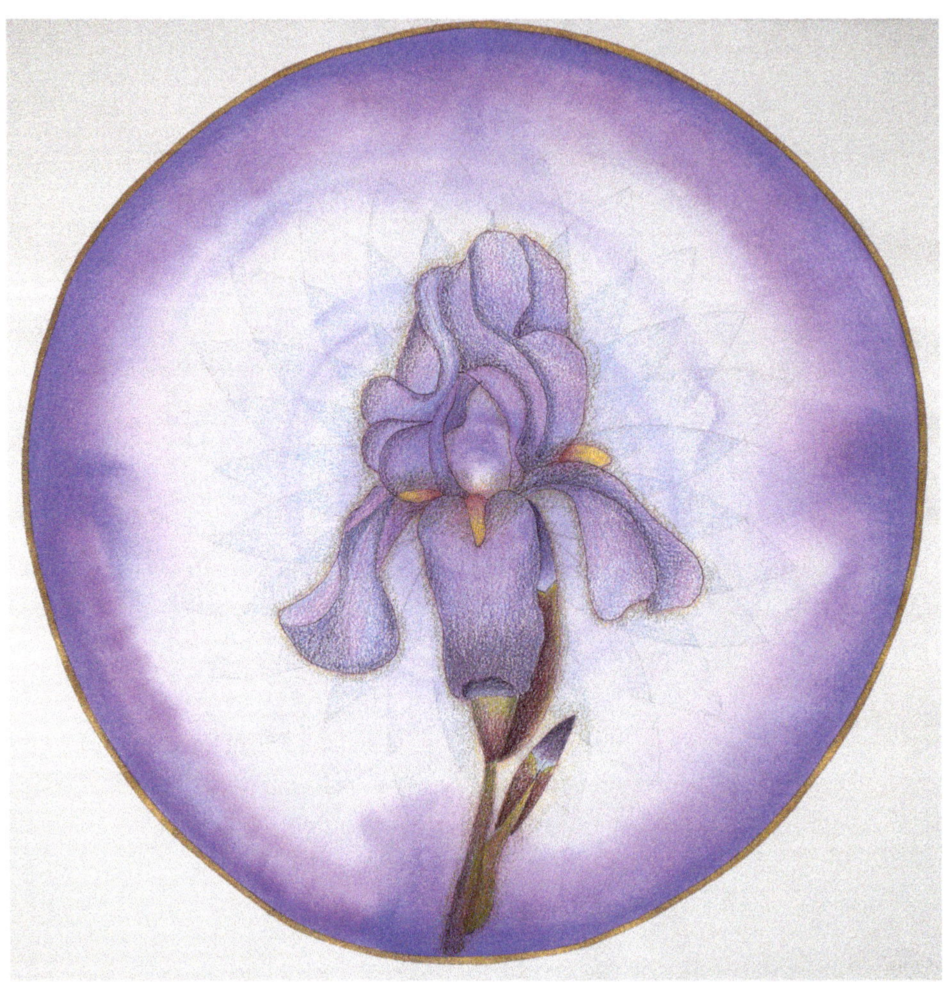

"Opening To Indigo"

Watercolor, colored pencil, gold ink, 22" x 22" 1998

Because I created this painting called "Opening Your Heart to the Gift of Autumn Color" (Part IV, pg. 73 "Use Color in Art to Receive Color's Gift") in a class I taught some time ago, it was important for me to remember the full significance of the painting when it was chosen for this book. St. Francis was the first teacher (whom I recognized) who came to me and whose words I transcribed. When he first spoke to me in my garden in 1987, the initial sign that he was there came when "Francis" appeared to be written across the top of my forehead. At first I really did not know which "Francis" it was. When I asked, the old fresco from Assisi, *St. Francis Preaching to the Birds*, popped into my mind. "Oh, <u>Saint</u> Francis!" I said, bursting into tears and feeling humbled, honored and not at all prepared for the visitation. An indigo-colored iris appeared in my mind and I took it to be a symbol of him. I asked why he had come. he said. I sensed he was to be my spiritual teacher and protector, and, by moving into the energy of the indigo iris, I could learn to be more like him, which would open my heart. Traditionally indigo is the color at the third eye or brow chakra, between the eyes at the forehead, and it is for connecting with one's higher self and intuition. *Opening to Indigo* was both a reminder of my commitment to my own spiritual opening, and that my teacher was always near, as he continued to tell me he was.

INDIGO: UPLIFTED IN GLORY

Thank you for this
wondrous gift, this glory,
as I sit among
the beautiful indigo
and reap her beauty.
What gifts
what joy,
I am honored.
I breathe you in
and I am surrounded
with hope and calm.
I am uplifted and glorified.
I know love, I know power,
the power of glorious love.
I am capable of loving
and my love is of God
and powerful
and grounded in the
heavens and higher realms.
You exist, don't you?
You are here—You are there.
I am dipped in hope,
uplifted in glory, fulfilled in love,
complete in the
knowledge

of the deeper truth
that God is joy
and is alive inside of me.
With you, my indigo
I am glorified,
I am filled,
I am uplifted,
I am whole and complete
in God's love
and I am love,
and I love with glory
because that's all I can do
when I am so full.
Indigo,
you so press upon me,
I can not turn away.
You have captured me
and pushed me forward,
upward
in fullness of joy
with an intensity
that I am weak to ignore.
I surrender,
I am happy to.
You have filled my heart,
you have filled my soul
and what overflows
is divine love.
I am divine and
you have reminded me
of my divinity.

Oh, it's so good to remember.
Thank you for your gift.
In your color I will not forget.
But, just in case,
thank you for being there
to remind me.
I welcome you into my
Bouquet of Life.
With indigo I am divine.

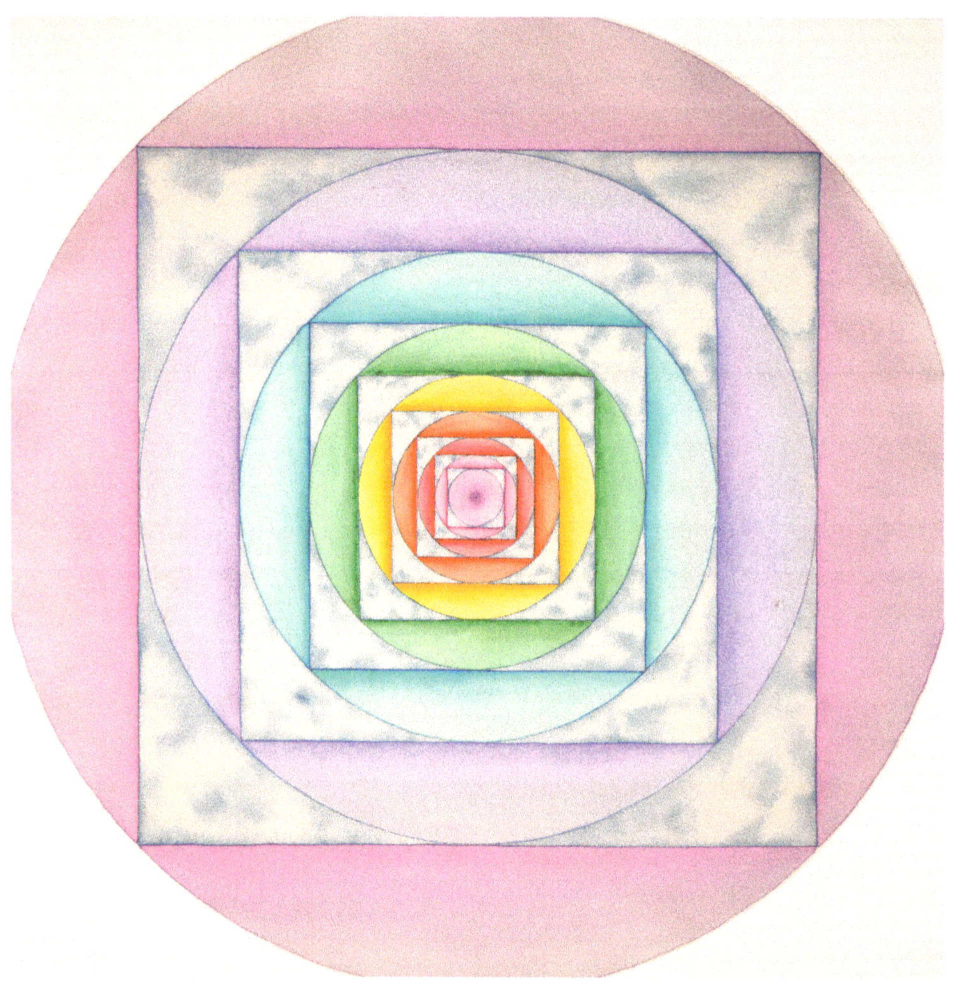

"FOR THE LOVE OF BLUE"

Watercolor, 22" x 22" 1999

For the Love of Blue was painted in a class called "Mandala Color Healing," and was originally intended to be a kind of color wheel. I always teach a section on designing a color wheel in my classes as a way to practice the watercolor washes, or techniques, which I demonstrate. A basic color wheel is mandala-like, circular and symmetrical around a central point and has the three primary colors (red, blue, and yellow) and the three secondary colors (orange, green, and violet.) Painting one is a great way to both learn how to create mandalas and to work with colors. Since I usually do the assignment alongside my students, and therefore have painted many color wheels, I like to challenge myself to come up with new designs which excite me. I have often said that if your work doesn't turn you on, what's the point of painting? My color wheels tend to be non-typical and not necessarily an exact, or true color wheel, meaning that every color is not always in its correct location to its opposite color. For me, pushing the boundaries and the rules allows for more creativity. *For The Love Of Blue* is one such design. Beyond that, I am fascinated with space and the infinity of blue sky and clouds and like to paint them in my mandalas. I find it to be very meditative and calming. So, in this mandala I got to do a lot of meditating! The title of this painting comes from the memory I had while painting it: that "baby blue" was my favorite color as a child, and that blue brought me a lot of comfort when I was young.

The Healing Of Blue

Blue is so calming and
soothing.
It's so quieting
and loving and comforting.
It surrounds.
Oh, what a beautiful gift
we have been given
with the sky,
with the calming of blue.
And the wind blows
and blows the thoughts
out of my head.
It cleanses me.
It soothes me.

It's forceful.
It wants my attention.
I am surrounded by love.
I am enveloped.
God is everywhere.
Surrounding me in air
and inhaling me
and I inhale God.
Glorious! This blue, this love,
this comfort, this calm,
I can relax and let go.
I can become blue
and then I am so alive,
alive in love.
My natural state?
Of course.
If I remember.

It's coming home.
It's welcoming.
Blue holds me in its arms.
Oh! Thank you.
I needed that.

But, you're always here.
Smiling, surrounding,
gentle, caring.
I am life with green,
I am love with blue.
It is a visitation,
this joy of color,
this God smiling
and knowing himself.

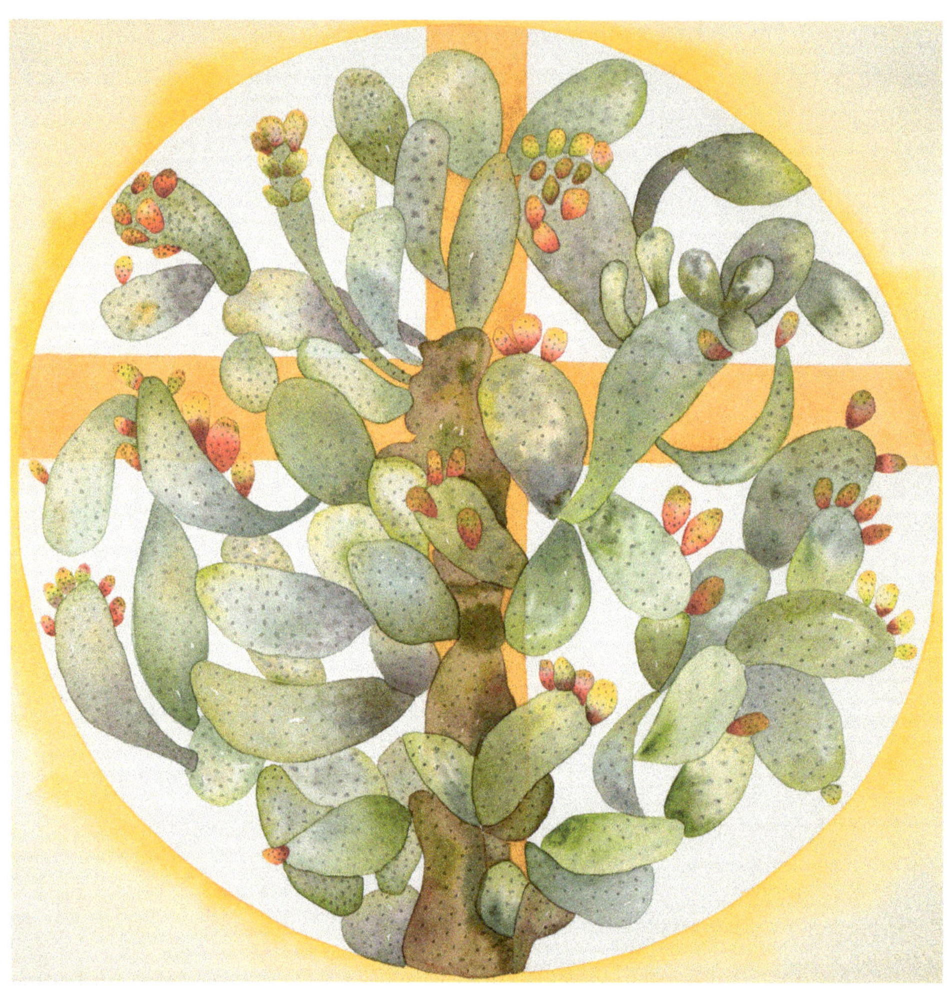

"Cactus Over Cross"

Watercolor, 15" x 15" 1999

This is a prickly pear cactus which is growing in the gardens of the California Mission San Juan Bautista, just outside the chapel of Our Lady of Guadalupe. It got my attention with its wonderfully expressive shape and the various greens accented with reds. The gardens have such a beautiful spirit and I have spent some peaceful days painting there. The day I painted this, I was with a group of like-minded friends who had gathered to paint, after first meditating together. It was a fantastic experience as we supported and held the energy for each other. I recommend painting with a group like this, especially if it's followed by lunch! The gold cross was the first thing I painted. It wasn't really there, but I saw it there. Then, over the top of the cross I painted the cactus, enjoying each leaf's shape, each shade of green, and its total uniqueness. At first it kind of surprised me to have this painting selected for the book. But, it is so full of smiles and has such a personality. It gave me a wonderful feeling diving into it, getting to know it, and then painting it.

Be Green! Green Said

Green is
hope.
Hope for growth,
for change,
for growth out of
soothing love.
About creativity,
about life,
life itself.
The sparkle and fizzle
of life itself.
Growing, bubbling,
magical,
reaching beyond itself,
smiling happily
to grow in the sun light.
Green needs the sun
to grow
to become itself.
Let the green in,
the growth
the joy
the hope
the smiles
God inside you.

Green is
God inside you growing,
loving you,
feeding you,
changing you,
evolving you,
ever more upwards,
ever more open,
to the love of self.
Enjoy green,
ingest green,
live green,
be green,
be God growing.

It's just opening
to God's love
and being it.
Let green course
through your veins.
It's just
God loving you.
Smile inside.
He is there. He is here.
Green on the outside
reminds you that God
is on the inside,
loving you, being you.
Smile.
God loves you,
self loves you,
love yourself
loving yourself.

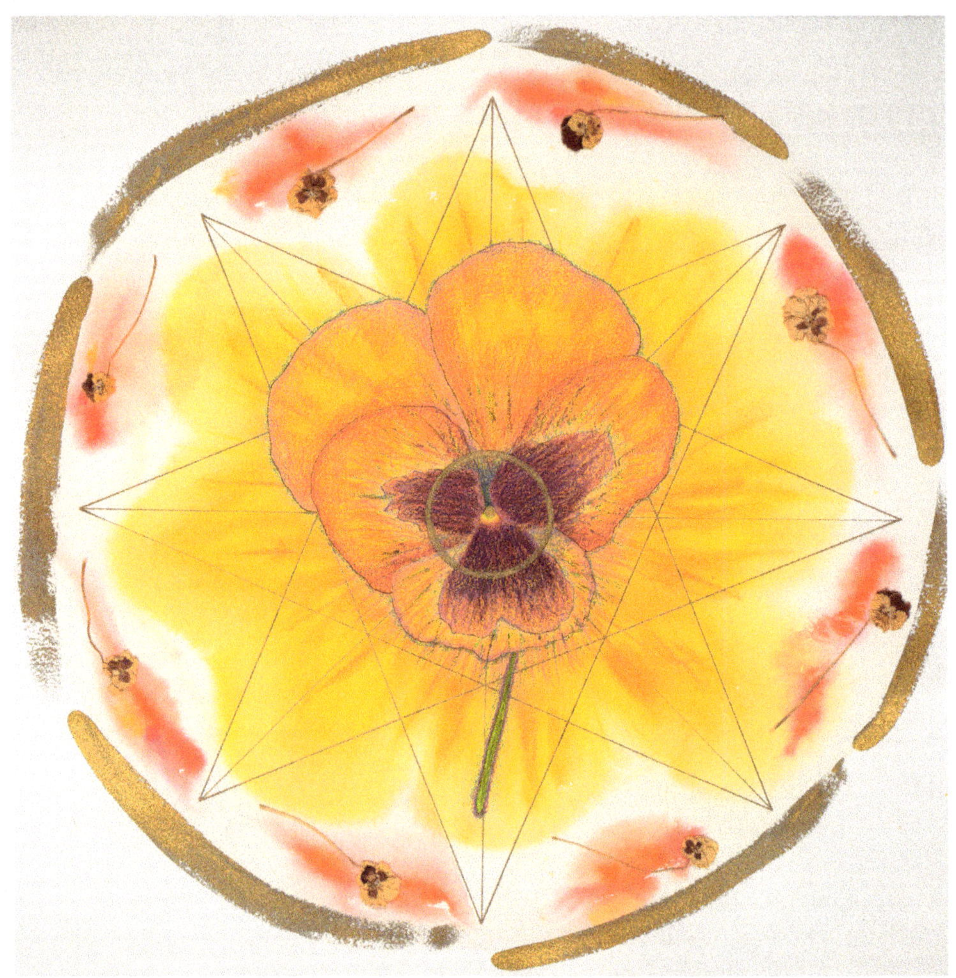

"Opening To Yellow"

Watercolor, colored pencil, gold ink, dried pansies, 22" x 22" 1998

    This, along with the indigo iris, was painted in the class "Open Your Heart to the Gift of Autumn Color." My intention was to open up to yellow and to deepen my already strong connection to it—yellow has always been one of my favorite colors, one I especially like to wear. I started by trying a new technique in order to push myself beyond my comfort zone. On a full sheet of watercolor paper which I squared off, I painted a large circle of plain water and then dropped various shades of yellow onto the wet surface. I let the colors randomly mix together and then dry. The next day I looked at the mass of yellow to see what image wanted to emerge, saw the pansy and drew it with colored pencils. It was actually with this painting that I first experimented with sacred geometry, and so I drew the eight-pointed star. I finished the piece by gluing on dried pansies which came from my garden

—— 40 ——

and added quick strokes of gold ink to complete
the circle. This was really a fun process and
more involved than I was used to. Prior to this
I would usually finish a painting in about two
hours. This new approach allowed me to focus
on yellow, feel it, think about it and to be with
it in my life for the entire week prior to the next
class meeting. During this time my appreciation
and gratitude for all colors grew immensely, as I
used this same painting technique for each col-
or we did in class.

YELLOW: THE GLOW OF GOD

From wherever you've been
in whatever time or place,
you've called to me, my yellow.
Bright, glowing, happy,
golden and warming
I have felt your warmth and your glow.
To be wrapped in your glory
has always been natural for me.
What is this I feel from yellow?
What treasures have you?

I am your strength
and your illumination,
your smiles and happiness,
your glow of golden power,
your belief that all is well.
For like the power and
warming rays of the sun,
you too can shine forth
and bring sunshine where it is needed.
Where the yellow shines
or where the sun shines,
upliftment and healing
are not far behind.
Yellow is about trust,
trust of the infinite warmth

and power and glory of God.
Life would not be,
without the yellows,
for they bring such power
to the peaceful serene blues
and bring you the green of life.
Notice wherever yellow shines its light
for it brings ancient wisdom
and the glow of love.
Glowing and illuminating
the glory of God's love,
could life be without it?
Would life grow upward
and be glorified?
Would you know the power
and glory of God?
Would you know what it would be
to be illuminated?
Would you know happiness
and its possibility in your life?
Could you feel the glow
in your being and smile
on the inside and on the out?
So, what is yellow you ask?
The power and the glory
and the smile of God.

So my little pansy, with its smiling face
and uplifted arms, glows and is glorified
as yellow, and touches me
with its glow so that I too, smile and glow
and am warmed and uplifted
and reminded that I can take in this
rich and warming color
and tingle and glow
with such happiness.
Thank you yellow, for what you do to me.
For, in you, I am glorified,
I am illuminated
and I am in
the Glow of God.

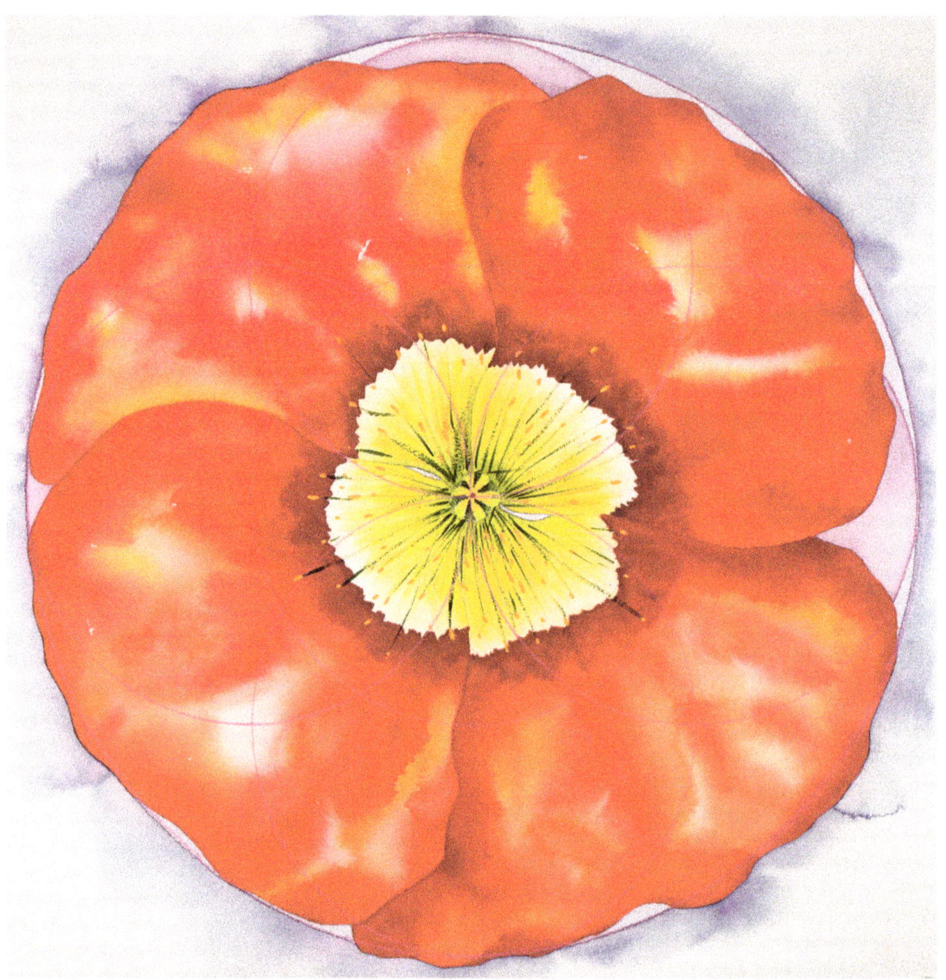

"Big Orange Poppy"

Watercolor, colored pencil, 22" x 22" 2000

This *Big Orange Poppy* is an Iceland poppy. I have grown them for years and marveled at both their strength and delicacy. They look almost like tissue paper and I once had a neighbor question why I was putting paper flowers in my garden! When my husband and I were first dating, we worked together in an office complex and shopping center which had gardens full of them. They were a new flower to me at that time, and I grew to love them because he was so fond of them. In a brochure he was commissioned to do for the site, he painted an orange Iceland poppy entwined with a pink rose for its cover, and it was our secret that these were a symbol of us together. He was the poppy, and I, the rose. I've tried a number of times to paint these poppies and have found them to be a real challenge. The orange ones have always seemed especially powerful to me. I painted this one as big as I could, I think to somehow understand its power and acknowledge the enormous significance this flower has played in my life. A friend's mother was visiting from Italy, saw the painting and was visibly moved by it. "Forte!" she exclaimed, meaning strong. It's kind of an "in your face" painting. I wasn't sure about it when I first painted it, thinking perhaps that it was just too much. But it usually elicits a smile, and being "too much" has sometimes been my own experience of orange. Over the top of the poppy, in colored pencil and barely discernible, is a design which is part of the "flower of life." The flower of life is a very ancient symbol made of nineteen overlapping circles which can be repeated infinitely. Flowers of life have been found at ancient sites all over the world, and both their meaning and how they got there remain a mystery.

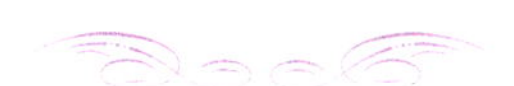

Orange: Divine Fire

The message of orange is
that it is so alive.
It moves and flows and ripples
just like fire, just like flames.
It is alive with potential and possibility
and curves and winds and smiles and glows
with teaming life.
Orange is life alive, pure, bright,
glowing, rippling, crackling with life
and creativity.
Orange is hot but it smiles
and lures you to itself
to explore the myriad
of its possibilities.
And, what are the possibilities?
Teaming with life,
it creates and it celebrates ever flowing,
ever moving, dancing and winding

toward the divine.
It shouts to you—
"Seek the divine, seek the power."
And what is that intense power but love?
Orange loves intensely but why shouldn't it?
It wants your attention. It's gotten it finally.
You see it, you feel it, you celebrate it
and you embrace the power,
the energy to create, to move,
to grow, to smile with delight.
For you have received
the glow of orange,
its spark,
and you understand divine love
in a new way.
It does not rest
until it touches you
and when touched,
you are smitten as never before.
For you are now alive
and on fire with divine love,
in your heart
and entire being.
Smile and celebrate,
can it get any better than this?

Thank you my divine orange
for lighting my fire.
May I not burn myself
with it!

Take orange into your heart
and embrace it and see it
from the eye in your heart.
And its heat
will make your entire being
glow with divine love
and divine life.
And if it burns at all,
it will be a Divine Fire.

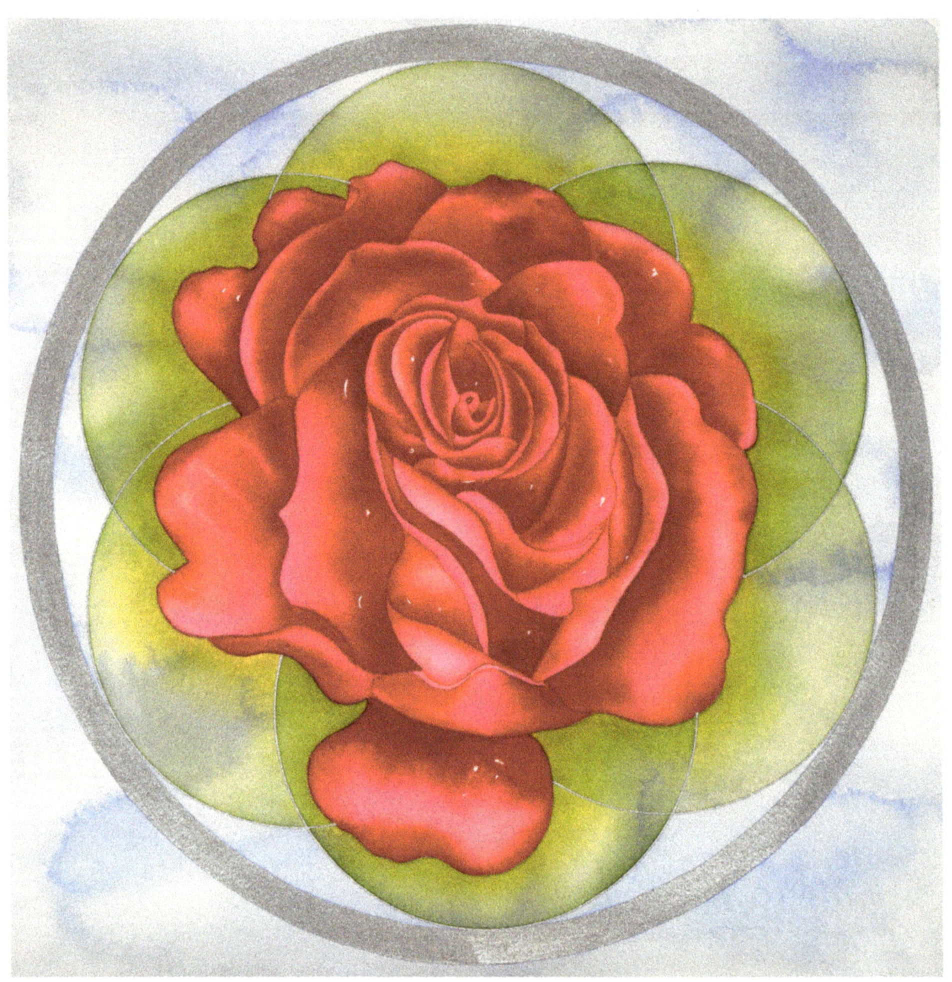

"The Rose In My Heart"

Watercolor, 15" X 15" 2001

I first saw the rose in my heart after my granddaughter was born. Following her arrival, I sat in my garden contemplating what a profound event her birth had been for me. Overcome with emotion, I saw a red rose in my heart on fire. It felt like my heart had never quite opened in the way it was opening with her birth. She is so special to me. She was born about six months before I began this book, and it never occurred to me that _that_ rose would be part of the book. As the book neared completion, there was only one painting I had left to do—a red flower. It had to be that red rose. I wasn't too thrilled about it either, it just seemed too emotional. As I finally accepted what I had to do, I kept having the feeling that the rose was to be painted at the Mission in San Juan Bautista. I went there twice in order to find and paint a red rose, and left both times not getting what I wanted, feeling frustrated, irritable and my body aching all over. The one painting I did was not what I wanted for the book; a bird left droppings on my paper, bugs swarmed me and I dropped my brush on the painting and red paint went everywhere. I was realizing that red was definitely a powerful color to work with, and it was working on me! Working with the red rose was stirring things up in me. It was bringing up my anger which I had hoped was being cleared. This inflamed my body and an old knot in my back behind my heart, which I have long known held the key to all my dis-ease, ached for days and then the pain softened, released and disappeared. I had been waiting for that for years. And then my granddaughter began saying her first words, and I saw her point to and say "flower" and my heart completely melted. She was just ten-and-a-half months old. How did she know that saying that word would be the key to my heart? She opened my heart and I could finally begin painting the red rose.

I painted the first layer of red in the rose (there are two, and in some places three, layers of red) and then had to go in for some dental work. That turned into an emergency root canal, another medical procedure I did not want! Not over the shock of that, the same day I was called and told that a suspicious cyst had been found in my breast and my HMO was scheduling me for a consultation with a surgeon. Now, try as I might, I could not keep fear from surfacing and I began to sink into a depression—I was so tired of being sick. I needed some powerful help fast, so I broadcast five paintings to myself, (see "Prayer for Broadcasting Paintings" in Part IV, pg. 74) with the intention of releasing fear, centering myself and staying connected to the God within. The next morning I felt much better, had no fear and felt strong and centered. That week I painted the next layers of red on the red rose and the first layer of the background. I actually amazed myself with this painting—it felt like I had stretched beyond what I thought I could do and was mesmerized by the rose's color and character. I hung it up so I could really let it talk to me. And, in between the next wave of events, I painted more layers of the background.

"You'd better take care," a healer friend said when he asked his guides about my cyst.

What did that mean? More fear surfaced. So I worked on myself using the Violet Flame as I had never done before." (See "Using the Violet Transmuting Flame" in Part IV, pg. 71.) My friend, and dowsing teacher who had taught me to use the pendulum, happened to call that afternoon and I asked if he'd dowse the seriousness of the growth. When he found it to be "serious and life-threatening," he began to send me healing energy.

"You're not going to believe all the violet light I'm seeing," he said. Even though he said I'd be okay, I could not stop the wave of fear nor talk myself out of it.

"So, this is what it feels like to face a serious illness," I thought.

At the very same time that this was happening, my mother-in-law suffered a mild stroke and was admitted to the hospital. My own fear turned to fear for her and then to anger when I felt I just couldn't deal with anything more. Within 48 hours, and not an easy 48 hours as I processed all this, we picked her up from hospital, all in surprisingly good spirits. My own fear was gone and so was hers. And, I was entirely fascinated hearing her tell me about the vision of colors and flowers she had seen for two days in the hospital—all in whites, reds and pinks! I thought about how the new life coming in, my granddaughter, was seeing flowers and the life passing on was seeing flowers. I was somewhere in between, working with flowers to open up my own vision.

Finally, when I went for an ultra sound, the technician, who would not or could not, tell me about the thing or nothing she saw on the screen, did say she saw me living beyond 100 years old. And then, in a brief and wonderful holy moment, she said, "Put your faith in God and all will work out."

She had confirmed something I had always felt—that I would be around for a long time. Her faith touched my own faith and I felt free. I breathed very deeply the rest of the day and all the chatter was gone from around my heart.*

I am in awe of the red rose. St. Germaine said this book would be a spiritual practice and a purification for me, and that is surely what it's been. I see how the red worked on me for an entire year—it needed to—and why this painting had to be painted last.

Here is something I discovered that my guide White Eagle said about the meaning of the red rose:

"The white rose stands for the pure and innocent spirit and the red rose for the spirit or soul of man after it has passed through the depths of human experience and learnt the meaning of love…Mankind is often stretched upon a cross in physical life, but as a result of crucifixion, the fragrant rose is born within him. The rose stands for the heart of love." (White Eagle, *Spiritual Unfoldment 1*.)*

The fire that I had seen around the rose in my original vision, in this mandala is the fire of love in the heart, and I painted it green—the color of the heart chakra. The green is in the shape of six overlapping circles, a piece of the Flower of Life.

*I did finally have a biopsy and it was on 9/11, *yes the 9/11*, while the radio somewhere in the background broadcast the news from New York. It was surreal! The biopsy turned out to be cancerous. That phase of my journey is on page 85.

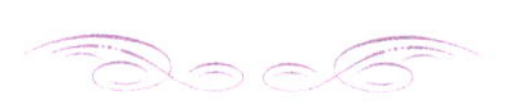

RED: THE POWER OF DIVINE LOVE

Red, your divine beauty
touches my heart deeply
and it is unfathomable.
Where are you taking me?
Do I dare surrender
and go with you?
I am heady
with ecstasy.
What is this divine bliss?

I am divine love,
made manifest
for you to see and recognize
and drink in the passion,
and know you are not alone.
You see,
I am hard to totally take in—
the beauty, the power, the passion
can be difficult to be with
and surrender to,
because it goes to a depth
of such divine power
that it must be taken in
in small breaths,
in small realizations.
Could you allow yourself
the realization that
you are inhaling divine beauty,
divine love,
and know that it is now
inside yourself?
It is real,
it is alive,
it is for you,
to love you,
to touch you,

to bless you,
to caress you,
and for you to feel beyond all doubt
that it is real.
Divine love
is in this red rose.
Does it hide itself well
or are you not fooled?
Has it touched you?
Are you speechless?
Do you want to express
what this divine color,
this divine beauty,
this divine love
has done to you?
Can you?
Is it possible?
Or, do you just smile
and know
that you have been touched
so deeply
that you can't fathom how deep
or where the feelings have penetrated.
It has made your heart warm
and your face smile
and your eyes gloss over
from ecstasy.

Red is powerful,
and the power is divine.
Let it in,
it is not to be ignored or dismissed
because it is too powerful
to understand.
It is divine love
and that will change you forever,
if you'll let it.
Are you ready for red?
Are you ready for love?
Are you ready for your heart to open?
If you are, my divine one,
breathe me in
and fear not.
For you will then know
Divine Love.

Thank you for persisting,
my divine beautiful red,
for reminding me of
the power, the passion,
the compassion of this
deep Christ-like love.
I know you are alive
and you have a purpose.
I am yours.

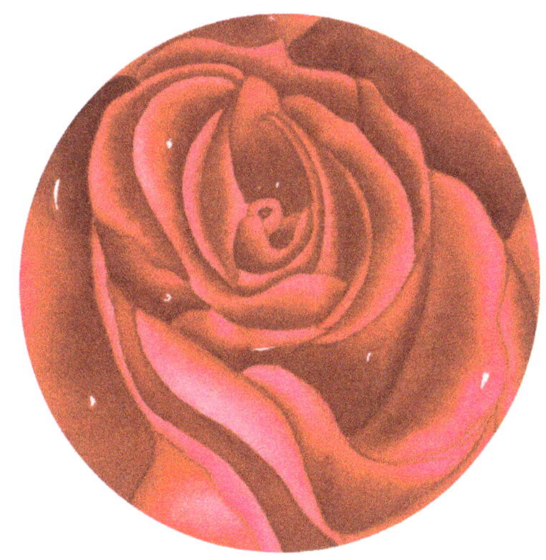

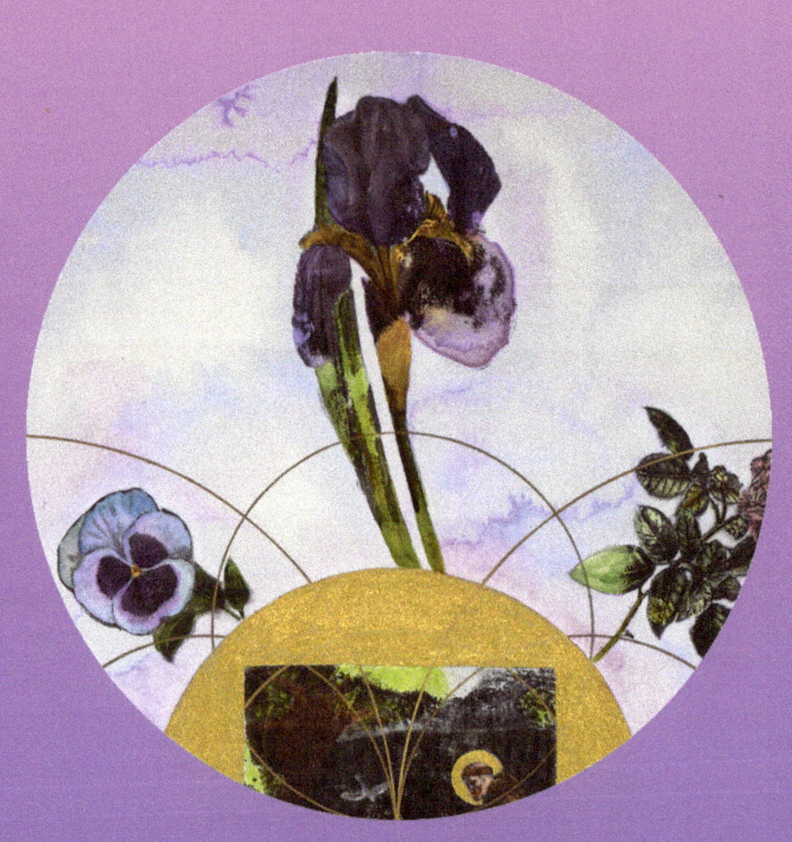

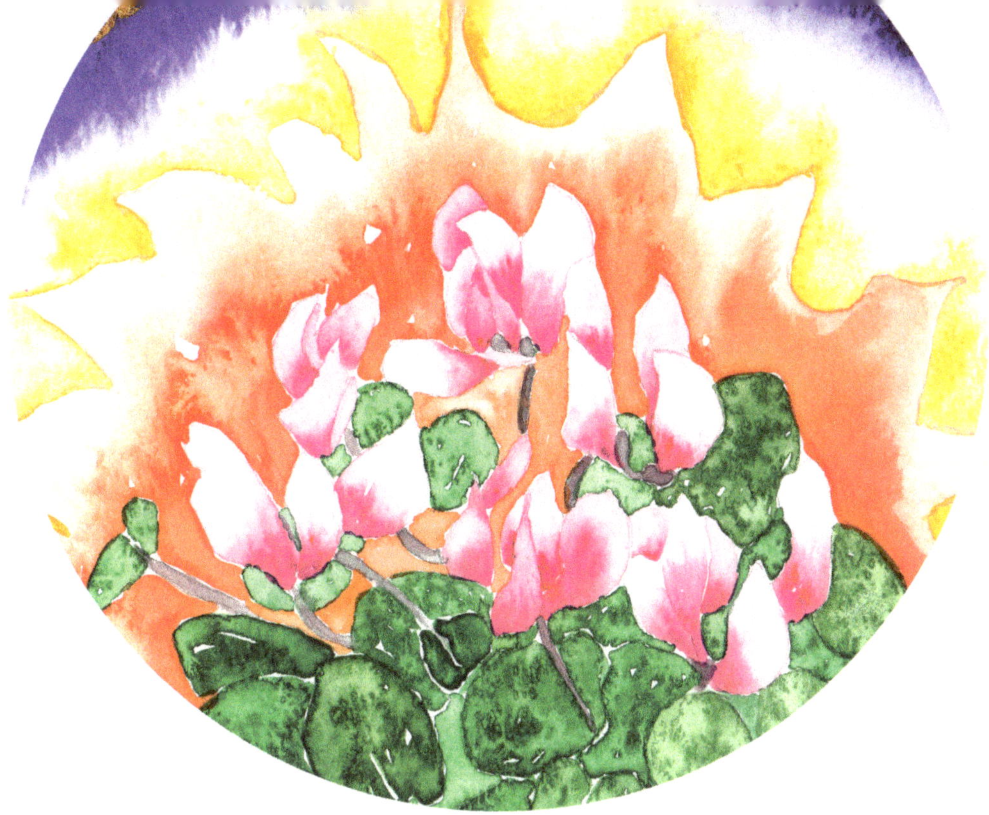

PART III

The Process Of Transformation:
Opening The Heart

It became clear to me that some of the mandalas which were chosen for this book were examples of my own process of transformation. Here the mandalas and messages are about releasing old emotions and patterns, and for me that was sometimes sad and painful as I acknowledged and faced parts of myself that needed to be released. Oftentimes, not understanding what to do next, fear or resistance would surface, and it was then that I would reach out to my guides for reassurance and help. Many times they would tell me: "fear not," or "all is well," or "we are always with you" and "we are here to assist." Over and over I would hear "follow your heart" and Part III is truly about just that. It is about clearing and releasing the old, opening to the new and moving from fear to love.

The Plan Of Transformation
A Message From St. Francis
August 30, 1998

I had a dream I was being killed and woke up and said, "I have to die to this life."

The journey to know myself has been a challenging one, as I imagine it would be for anyone. It can be a huge transformation and is often bigger and entails more than we expect. For me it required much letting go of the past, and that brought up more grief than I expected it would. I can see now it was all a necessary part of the process. But, during one particularly dark day I asked, "What's happening St. Francis?"

Fear not. We are near. And you are in our care. Listen closely for we will talk to you in the silence. All is well. You are being cared for. Let it in and let it happen. Let go to us—to the angels on high who surround you. For you have asked and it is being given unto you. What are you being given? Graduate status. The old ways are going and the new ways are being ushered in. It is all happening as it should. Be not afraid. But keep a close ear to us. For you are part of the plan. The plan of transformation—and that is what is happening to you. Observe it carefully. For much is happening to you and around you. The frequencies are changing and that is affecting you deeply as it should. Stay aligned to the higher realms for that is how you will survive and shed your old skin and your old ways and come to totally embrace and Be the New. The New is totally attuned and aligned with the higher realms. You are still struggling to hang on to some of the old. This gives you the struggle. Let go and the struggle and hardships will lessen. Embrace the New—the Higher Vibration —and you will be a happier person.

We love you and await
your reaching for the light.
You do not need to stay in the darkness.
Go play now!
St. Francis

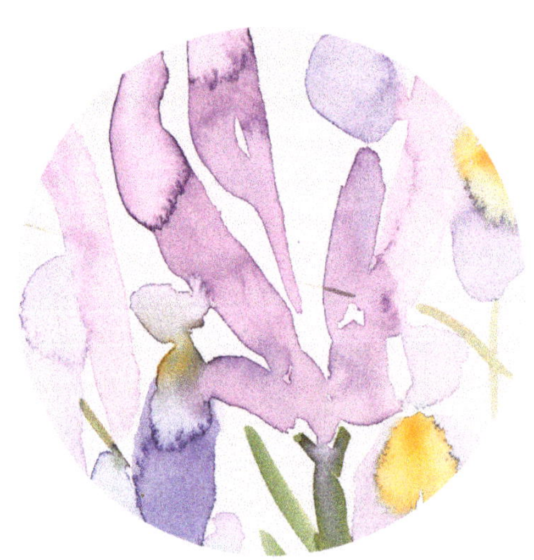

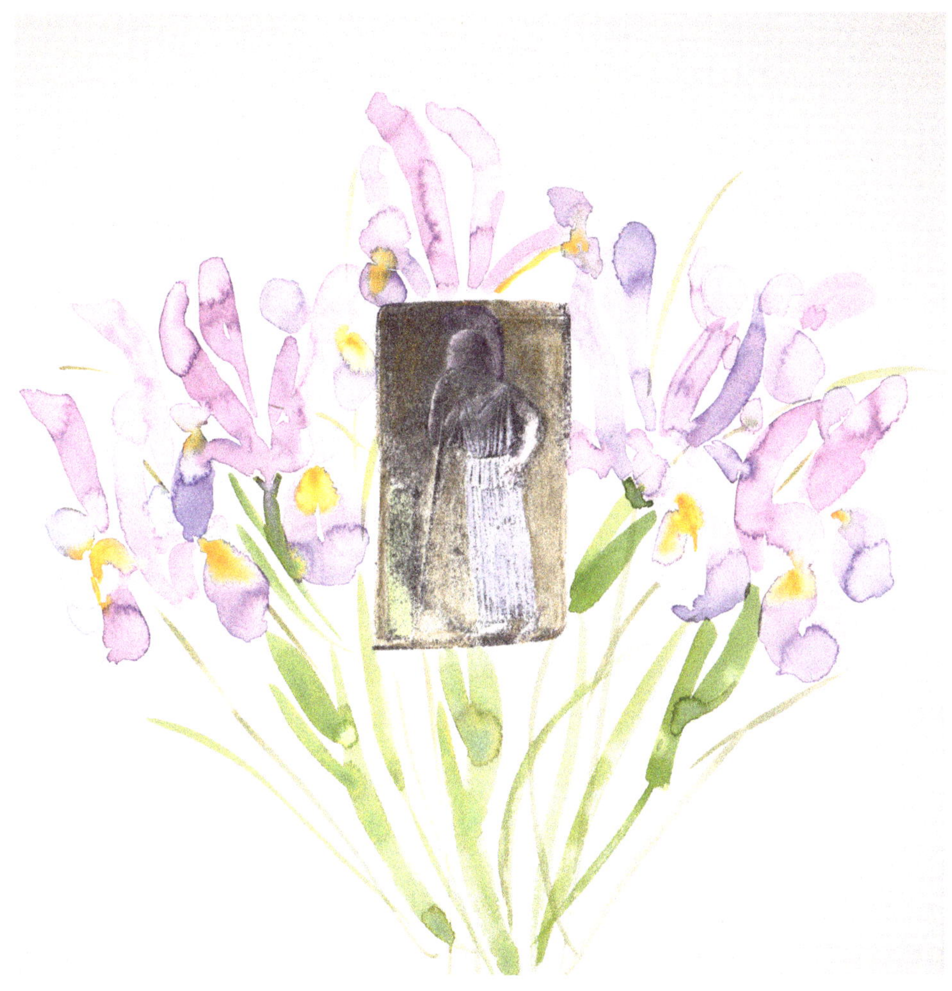

"Mourning"

Watercolor, ink transfer, gold ink, 15" x 15" 1994

I had long identified myself with Athena, the Greek goddess. I was tough and held high ideals, like she did. Some called me "aloof" in high school and I didn't feel like a "sweetness and light" person. The image of Athena in this painting is not as an invincible warrior, but in a state of mourning. She embodies sorrow. I strongly identified with this representation of her in my life at the time. Sometimes I thought I was falling apart, and in retrospect, I was. I had to. If I was committed to opening my heart, the protective shell had to go. I saw this painting as a funeral marker, bringing flowers to the grave of a death of a part of me. But it was also a celebration. The bouquet of irises seemed to be a symbol of new blossoming. I was acknowledging a death, but opening to a new life, and in the spirit of the iris. My intention was to paint within a circle format, so I loosely consider this a mandala.

"Diving Into The Cyclamen"

Watercolor, gold foil, 11" x 11" 1996

A beautiful pink cyclamen gave me a nudge I had needed for a long time. I'd wanted to create a class called, "Painting Nature, Painting Self" and painting this mandala was a way to try out the assignment for myself and see what the experience would be for my students. The idea for the class was to find elements in nature we were attracted to, paint them into mandalas and see what nature was mirroring about ourselves. My own intention in this case was "Diving into the cyclamen to know it, understand it and to receive from it," which was written on the back of my paper before I began. As I painted the flowering plant, I felt that I touched deeply into its energy and to my own. But I wasn't prepared for what I received—the message I got about pink. I've always felt I had a kind of love-hate relationship with pink. I'm glad it set me straight, because in truth, I loved that pink flower. I think pink may really be my savior.

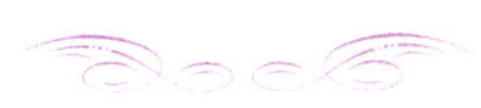

DEEP IN PINK:
REMEMBERING WHO YOU ARE AND WHY YOU ARE HERE

What is the message of this pink,
of this flower as it spirals
upward to the heavens?
Why do I want to dive deeply into you?
What have you for me?
I want to know your secret, the beauty in you
that appears so sweet, nurturing and kind.
The pink of sweetness draws me to you,
and I want to know who you are.

I am your sweetness reflected back to you.
I am your kindness, I am your loving nature,
pushing up toward the sky,
not to be forgotten, not to be ignored.
Oh, do you feel a bit vulnerable
in this soft side of yourself
being discovered?
Fear not, I will not tell, but in fact,
that pinkness is strength,
a kind of soft strength you are now
only just discovering in yourself.
Did you not really know it was there?
Did you not really know it's
the truth of you?
It has always been hard to accept,
this softness, this sweetness,
this vulnerability
that when you happen upon it once again
you have often said,
"Oh, no, not this again."
This is the color of your loving heart.
This is at the core of you, and you need it
as it needs you, to heal you, to love you
so that in your fullness, your heart spills forth
the love, the sweetness, the softness,

the nurturing and the pink.
Why are you attracted to pink?
You are not immune to the need
to be loved and nurtured,
of being softened by pink,
of being smiled on by pink,
of being completely touched by pink.
Are you? We hope not,
for when your heart is full of pink
it is soft and fluffy, and the absence of pink
just makes the heart hard.
Why do you want to dive into pink? Why not?
Why not be surrounded in the love
in the nurturing, in the sweetness?
Why not become
love, nurturing and sweetness?
It is who you really are. Do you remember?

Oh, I remembered. And then I forgot,
or did I simply forget to remember
or did I not really want to remember?
It matters not now, for I am here, in the pink
and remembering.
And remembering to remember
that I need the pink,
and the pink needs me to remind ourselves
who we are, and why we are here.
To know love, to know softness,
to know sweetness,
to open our hearts to pink
and never forget again.
So my dear cyclamen,
thank you for being my torch,
my soft flame of love.
Now let me stand tall like your pink flame,
in my strength, which is my softness.
And thank you pink,
for reminding me who I am.
For in you I am strong, gentle, open. I am love.
Wanting to dive into you
is really wanting to dive into my own heart.

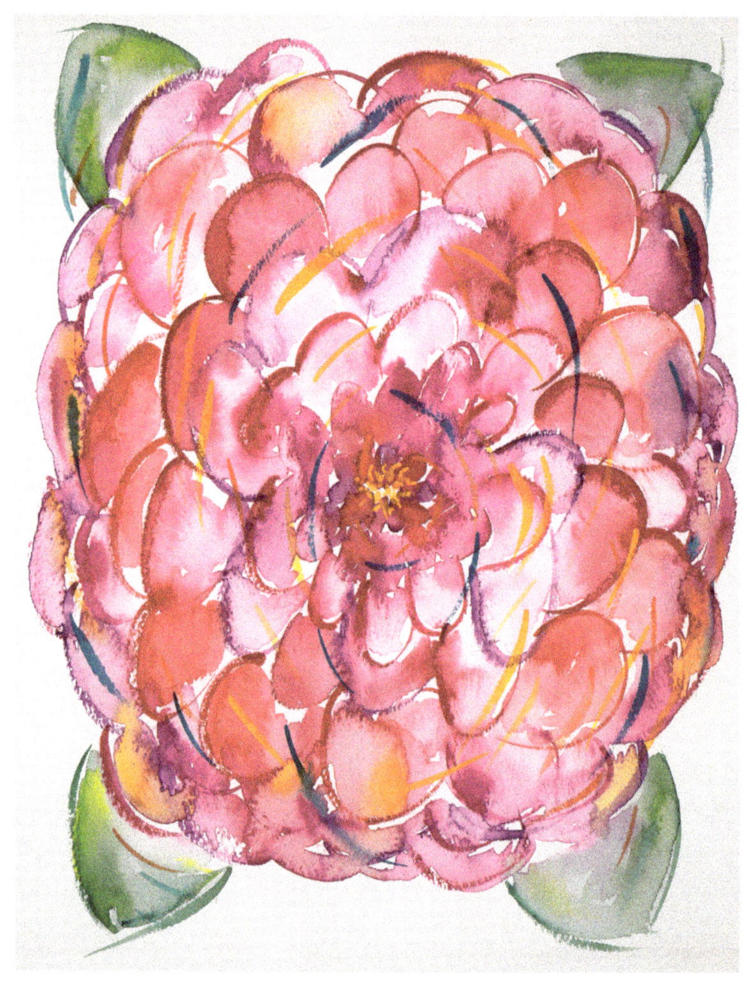

"My Self As A Flower"

Watercolor, 11" x 15" 1997

This painting was done in class. The assignment was for each of us to see ourself as a blooming flower. It was one of the first assignments I always gave in my classes to help students see themselves as a mandala, which most flowers are. The blooming flower is often used as a symbol of the unfolding spiritual self. Having done this many times before, I decided to let go, get playful and wrote this as my intention: "My self as a flower, having fun, loosening up!" I painted what I felt from my center, the colors and spontaneity were straight from my heart. It was so freeing. Having followed the shape of the paper when I was painting, this imaginary flower, wild and free, was not exactly a perfectly round circle or mandala. I like to remember this side of myself, because my tendency, especially when stressed, is to tighten up and try to be perfect. This was heaven for me, to be loose and free.

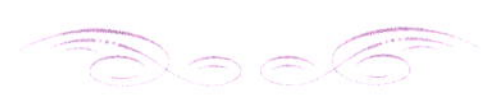

Follow Your Heart
A Message From St. Francis & St. Germaine
April 17, 2000

Because so much of my guidance was coming from the unseen, I felt the need for regular reassurance and some kind of signposts to tell me that I was on the right track, especially before this book was started. The destination of where it was going was really a mystery to me and sometimes my trust in the process got shaky. Here's what I asked one day as I tried to do the right thing:

Dear Guides,

Please assist and guide me as to what direction or continuation is next. Do I continue with the "Flower Energy Paintings," learning about color, light and form? Do I also pursue flower paintings which heal?" Please advise, clarify, help focus.

My Dear One,

We are here to assist and, as we've always said, are always ready to help when called on. You are doing just fine and flowing nicely in your life's path. Do not be threatened. All is well. We are with you and hear your request for clarity and we are glad to oblige. Watch for the Light, follow the Light, and your heart, and you will know where to go. You are going through much clearing, much needed clearing, and we assist as we are called on and as we are able. This process is a big one, and not to be taken lightly. You know this and you are proceeding bravely and well. We commend you. Your heart is in your flowers, and has always been, as well in the colors and light that surrounds them and you. Follow your heart and you will always do well and the "right" thing. Be in love, be with love and your heart will open and sing the love that is within. This is where you need to go, and you will go, automatically. Fear not. All is in order. Your lesson here is about letting your heart sing. So, you must learn to follow it, open to it, express it and revel in the totality of the love. It is glorious. Follow the love, and you follow the All. Follow the love and you follow the Way to all life and all healing, the All That Is. This you must choose yourself and GO. The way is open, but you must follow the path, the road signs, the hints, the clues, and find the treasure yourself. And, the treasure you will find will be the love in your own heart. Isn't that something! It is Within! So, that is why no one knows your path but you. You must be awake and aware. You must be ready. You must desire it and take the steps toward it and it will be yours. You MUST know your own heart. This is what we meant when we said, "Go on a Treasure Hunt in Your Heart." For it is there you shall find who you are and what you love and in loving that, you shall find it All. Hard to believe sometimes isn't it? But it is there that the truth lies and in embracing it, it will set you free. It is in finding your center, and loving that, that you shall find that you are connected to the All. So, you must explore your own heart, your feelings and emotions to know who you are and how you are a part of the All. It is most beautiful and we welcome your exploration.

So, in looking for your direction, follow your heart and the love, and not ever the "shoulds" or the "ought-tos." There is no love there—and this is what you're wanting to connect with. The Spark of love and light of God. You are finding it, and you now know to search deeper within. Within your own heart.

We bless your search.
The search for truth, love and light.
Your guides, St. Francis, St. Germaine & the All

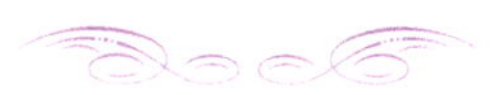

WE ARE ALL ONE
A MESSAGE FROM ST. GERMAINE

A few nights before New Year's Eve, 1999, an image came to me in a dream. It felt like it came out of the back of my neck, an area which is thought by some to be a new *chakra* (energy center) the pons, or the Mouth of God. The image was of a plant, with many large, bluish-green flowing leaves, all coming from one center, and rooted in the earth. The leaves moved and flowed independently in the gentle wind and it was very peaceful. I knew in the dream that this was to be a symbol for New Year's Eve, as we crossed into the new millennium.

And, so, on that much awaited eve, I participated in the world event by painting the image of the plant. I felt like it was something I had to do. I watched the beautiful world-wide celebrations on television with one eye on the screen and the other on my painting. I spontaneously began to chant an American Indian chant about unity. This seemed to help the paint flow and assist in the expression of the deep feelings I was experiencing. I was so moved by the lovely ceremonies, dancing, singing and celebrations which were being televised from everywhere on the planet and my heart opened. The green plant I was painting then began to change. I started to add one color after another, all in soft pastel colors. The single-color plant was transforming and unfolding into a multi-colored flower. Each color I added seemed to represent a nation, a people, their love added to the whole. And I loved them all very deeply. We were all a piece of the whole, a piece of the peace.

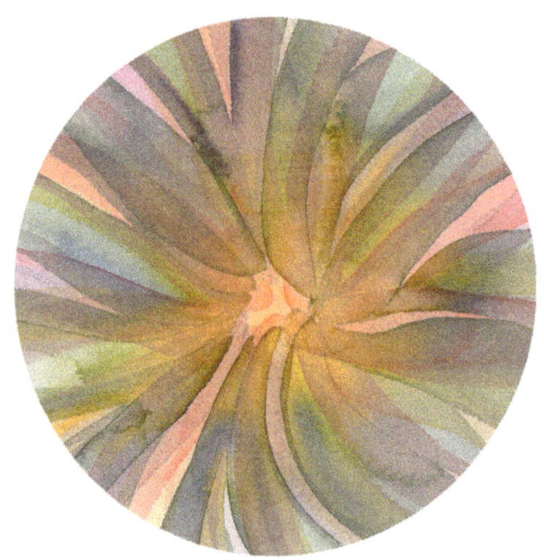

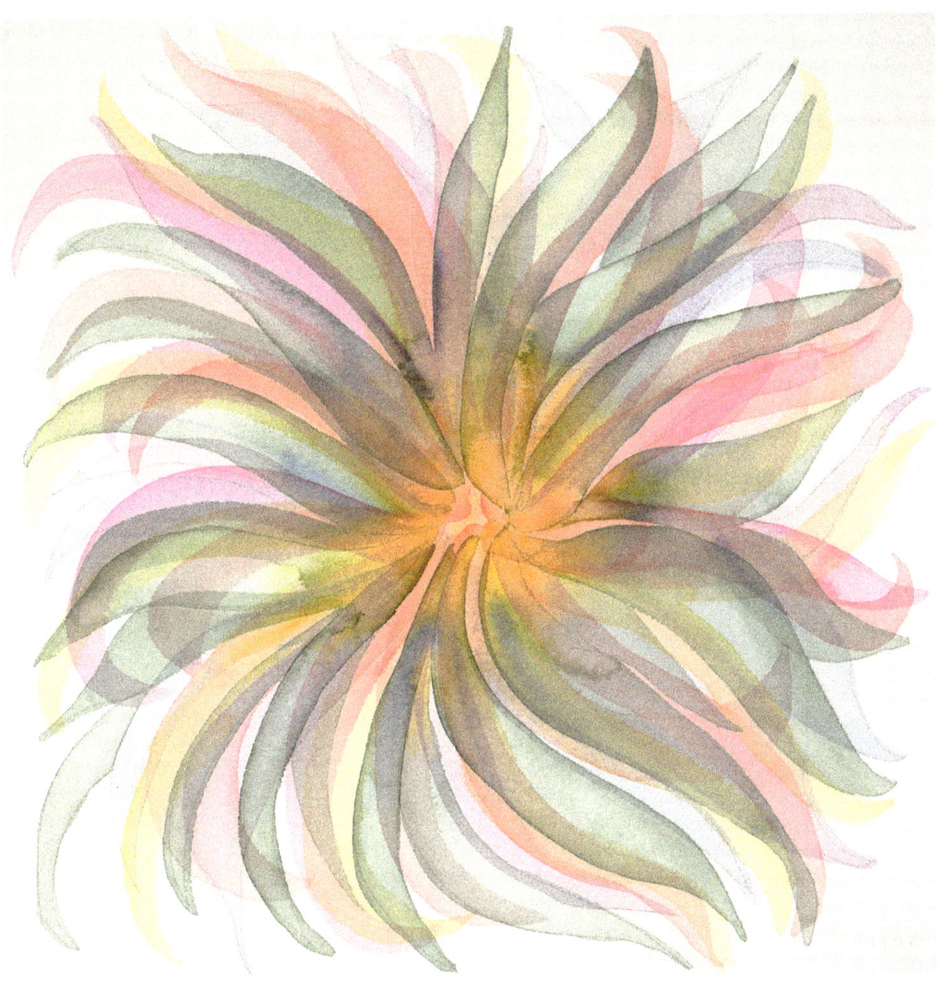

"Unity"

Watercolor, 15" x 15" 1999

The technique used in this painting is one of layering transparent washes, "washes" being how watercolor is applied. In order to have crisp shapes of transparent color over other colors, the paint must dry before additional colors are applied—otherwise you get a muddy mess. "Muddy" is what our relations with each other have sometimes become. However, when I look at this flower I feel the tremendous love I felt the night I painted it, giving me such hope for our planet and the future we could create. We can all sing together, dance together, flow together and live in peace together. And, like the plant, we can all be individual beautiful leaves while being part of the whole. Originating from one source, we are one. The lovely plant became an even lovelier flower, one of living love and energy, a symbol I believe, of not only our future potential, but our potential now.

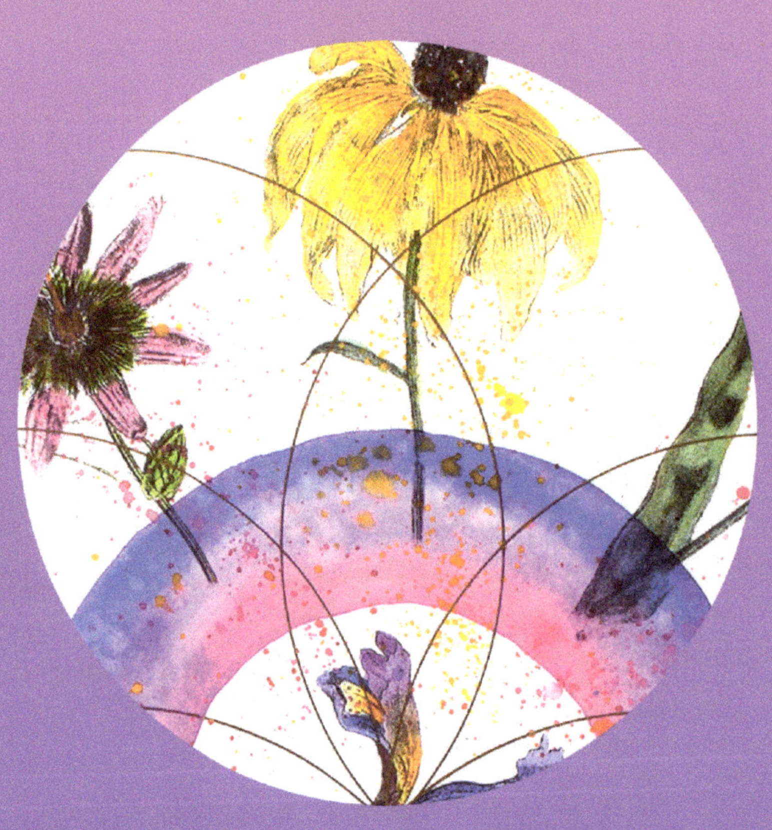

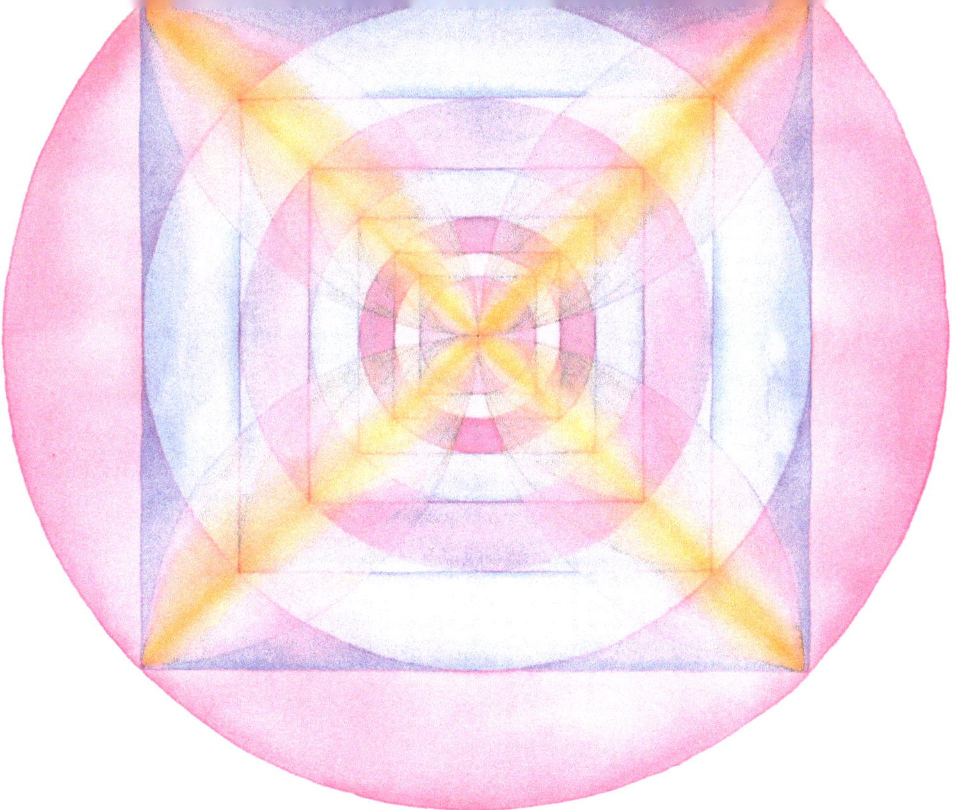

PART IV

Tools For Personal Transformation

Techniques, Suggestions, Lessons

This section is a compilation of many messages I received from various sources which were given to me as tools. I felt that they could be beneficial to others and offer them here for your use. I learned early on that in order to receive the messages, it was best for me to sit in a spot I discovered in my garden where I could feel the energy flow to me easily. I called this my "power spot." Additionally, as I wrote, I held a chunk of smooth amethyst crystal, which helped me feel connected to spirit and gave me confidence to receive and write down what I heard.

The messages here include using color for opening the heart, healing, and energizing oneself. There are wonderful lessons about flowers and how to connect with nature in new ways for balance and healing. You'll find techniques about how to create your own reality with love as well as how to create a sacred union with your spiritual guide. It is here that I share how I discovered that St. Germaine was my spirit guide, and how others can discover their guide or guides and know their names. Besides being fun, the fact is that our guides have been waiting for us to open up to them so that they can give us their wisdom. In the conclusion of this section there is an illustration of a pastel color wheel made with flower petals, and instructions on how to create one yourself. The final tool is for creating a personal mandala.

Blessings and joy to you as you begin your work—as we begin our work—together.

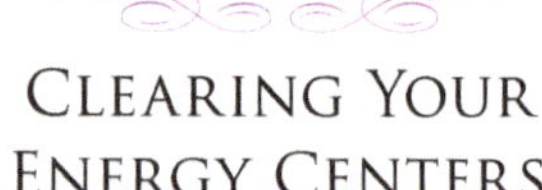

Clearing Your
Energy Centers
A Technique From St. Francis
August 11, 1987

This message came to me in the early stages of learning to listen, receive and write down guidance, and the words of St. Francis were the first I transcribed. The day I was given this technique I was experiencing some blockages in my energy, and when I asked for help this is what I was given to do. I try to use this daily. I start my meditation by connecting my feet to the center of the earth, bringing up earth energy and breathing it into my heart and then my body. I breathe in energy from the celestial realms as well. I want to clear and connect before I begin my day.

You are cleansed now. Your blockage has been burned away and your centers are once again flowing freely. This technique may be used anytime when a chakra* center gets blocked. Center into the earth in your power spot. Ask for your guides, counselors and guardians to help and be with you. Use your crystal, too. Pull the energy up from the earth. Wherever the energy stops is where your blockage is. You must burn it out. Start a fire outside yourself and put the blockage into the fire. Let it burn and burn until you can feel your energy starting to move and rise. See the next color it moves to—until you can move it out from the top of your head and on to infinity. See your chakras aligned and full of pure white light—completely clear so that you have a pure straight ray of light flowing up through your center. When this energy has continued to move up for a while and you feel good and clean and pure, close it off above your head. See your feet planted deeply in the ground as roots of a giant oak tree going forever into the Earth. Spread your arms up to the sky like branches of the oak, which reach to the sky forever. Breathe and expand your trunk and see yourself stable between sky and earth. Surround yourself with a large clear tubing so that no negativity comes in but you can exude your love energy out. Feel how pure and beautiful you feel and how connected to God. This is how we want you to practice feeling. This connection—this purity of heart and soul. For it is from this place that you will do your work. Stay clear. Stay pure. And learn to do this cleansing as you need to. You can take care of yourself. You simply need to know how to reconnect with God. Call on us anytime for help. ANYTIME. For we want you to stay as centered as you can, most, if not all the time. Yes, we know this is a big task. But, we know you can do it, and we know you have the desire, so that does not make it hard at all!

We love you so dearly and look forward to when you fully realize the true love you have in your heart, and accept it.
We bless you,
St. Francis

*Chakras are Sanskrit for spinning colored energy centers in the subtle light body.

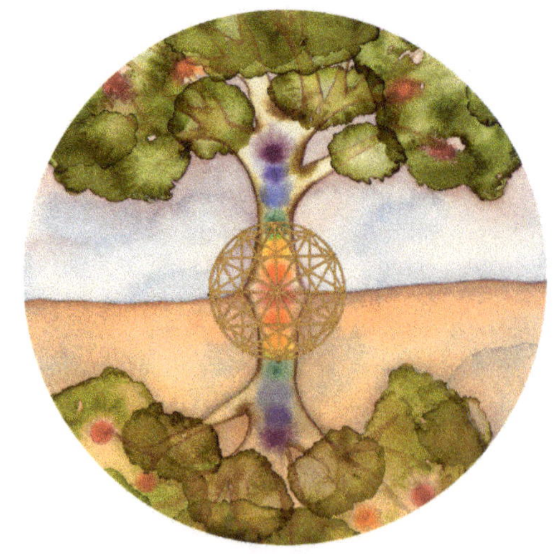

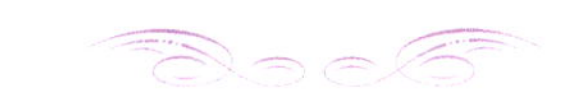

Bring Your True Nature Into The Light
A Suggestion From St. Francis
March 7, 1988

Through the years I have tended to hide my artwork, either under the bed or in the closet. Because it was so deeply personal, putting my work out to the world felt very vulnerable to me. I have felt the same about bringing out my true self. This message from St. Francis can really speak to any of us who tend to keep ourselves small when it's time to stand up and bloom. The message also reminds us that there is so much help available if we would ask. Besides the following, I got many offers of help in response to my asking. This included other messages from Van Gogh, who said he'd help with my painting technique so I could express my love of God. I was also offered help from all my female guides who wanted to help with my rebirth. For any of us to be who we really are, we can't leave our work or ourselves in the closet! The following was in response to questions about my work.

These paintings represent the beginning of your blossoming and should be honored. They are of nature and represent your true nature. Each one is a segment of the whole and represents a segment of you. They should not be kept in the dark, as flowers must see the sunshine to grow—as you must stay in the light to grow. Hiding them away is like hiding parts of your SELF away. And the whole needs all of its parts. Not even one small part must be kept hidden for it would affect the whole. So therefore, it is a balance of the sum of the parts—without one part missing—that is for the blossoming of the whole. I can help you bring your true nature out and not leave it hidden. To bring it out into the open—to the light. This hiding—this holding back of self—keeping it in the dark, can no longer be done. You know this. You have been afraid, guilty, self-pitying and lazy. Wake up. Stop avoiding the issue. Shine light on the subject. Time to face the issue of why you came here. Discovery of self. It will be such a lovely discovery—you have been fearful and yet as you experience it, it will be so surprisingly beautiful. Do not fear seeing a beautiful you—for this is what you will find.

We bless you deeply from the
depth of the essence of the love rose,
St. Francis

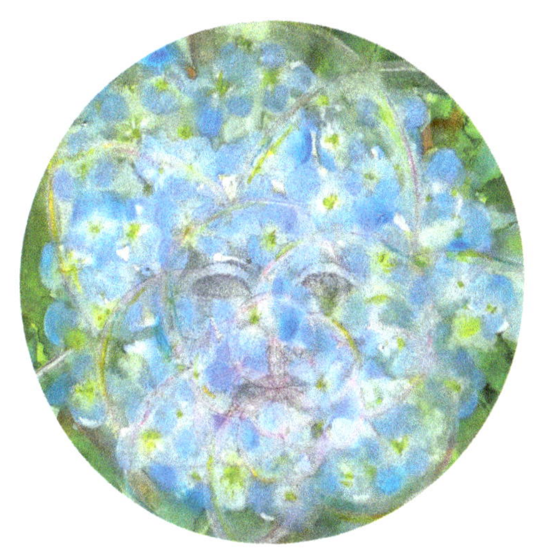

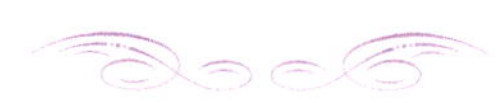

Enter The Flow Of The Universe Through The Plants

A Technique From St. Germaine
November 26, 1996

In meditation, when I asked how I could learn more about color, I saw the little purple violas I had just purchased, and sensed they were somehow the doorway to the knowledge I wanted. I sat with them in my garden before planting them and got the words, "Kingdom, another kingdom. This is the doorway in." I thought about the Hyemeyohsts Storm (Plains Indian teacher of the Medicine Way) workshop I'd recently attended, and he said we could ask any plant or flower we were drawn to, to heal us. When I allowed myself to do that, I felt I could go into the plant's world and be on its level. And that's when everything changed for me. I entered that world and it seemed that God was everywhere loving me; flowers and plants were a doorway to other kingdoms.

Call on me. I can provide answers and give you guidance. Keep following the light. Keep following the colors. Did you notice how you felt handling the plants? This is energy coming through—nature's energy. You were renewed, charged. Green renews—and now you wait for the blossoms, the combination of colors, the beauty, the truth. It is there, just wake up to it. There is much to tell you—they will tell you. Be open. Stay with the flow. Don't turn away by filling your mind with useless details that you worry about. Let go of the worry and fill your mind with love and light and color—useful thoughts! From the plants, you can enter the kingdom of God.

You can enter the flow of the universe.
You can let go of the never-ending
wheel of life that goes round and round.
You can enter the flow.
St. Germaine

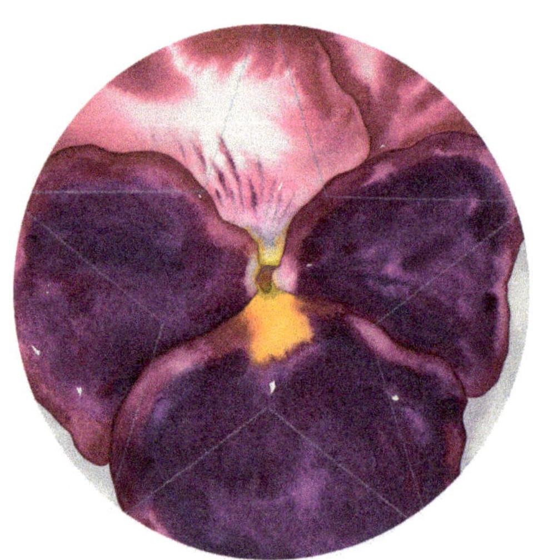

Prayer For Broadcasting Color

A Technique From my Teachers

When I do color work, and visualize send-ing color to help and heal myself or others, it is called "broadcasting." I begin by asking for the color which would be most beneficial and appropriate for the person at that time. The col-or appears in my mind and then I broadcast it by visualizing the color around the recipient. In broadcasting, I always include the intention for what the color is to be used for, such as bal-ance or peace, or clearing etc., and include this prayer. I fill in the blanks by hand and then read the poem aloud as if the person were in front of me. This prayer was given to me by my teachers.

(Person's Name)
(Intention)
My dear angelic being of light,
I broadcast (color) to you
for you to open your heart
and receive the healing light
and energies
of this magnificent ray of God,
to bless you,
support you,
love you,
so that you may know
of your own magnificence,
accepting yourself as you are
in its wonderment,
knowing that
within you
is the All That Is,
all color,
all light,
flowing in perfect harmony.
Thank you.

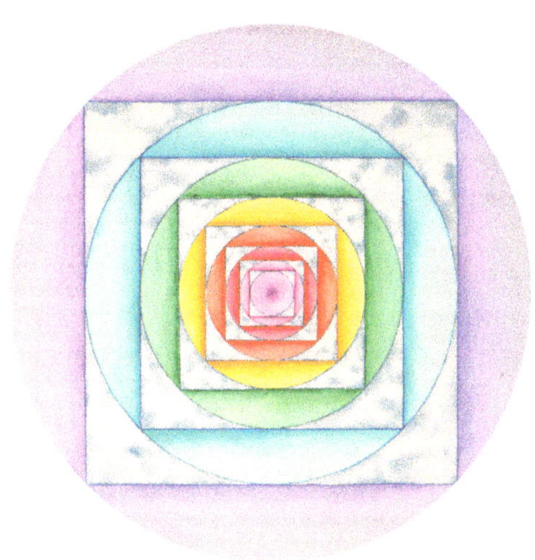

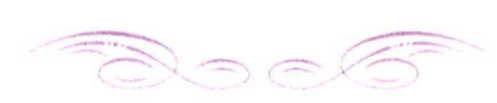

Surround Yourself With The Essence Of The Rose

The symbolism of the rose is profound and its essence is very healing. As aromatherapy, the rose vibration is the highest of any flower. Here is an early and most beautiful message suggesting we drink in the fragrance of the rose as the fragrance of God. The rose has always been so calming to me. At the time I received this, I was not familiar with White Dove, but her energy was so soothing that I certainly welcomed it as well as her lovely message.

We bring you Peace and the Peace Rose. Peace, Peace, Peace. Breathe in the lovely fragrance of the rose and center in—focus. Bring in your energy. Don't scatter it. Protect yourself—surround yourself with the essence of the rose. Keep your invisible protection strong. The rose scent will bring you peace and serenity. It will remind you of the love of God within—not without. Focus in. Center in. Go inward. Open to the love of God. The beautiful sweet fragrance. Surround yourself in this essence. The love of God. Keep it strong. Bathe in it. Use it as your armor. Both to keep yourself from becoming scattered, and from letting the energy that is not compatible with yours into your aura. The essence of Peace. The Rose. The true Christ. Blooms with the love of God. The Christ is the God-Self blooming. The symbol is the Rose.

Peace, Peace, Peace.
Spread peace in every way you can,
but first by spreading it
and carrying it around yourself.
We love you and send you PEACE,
White Dove

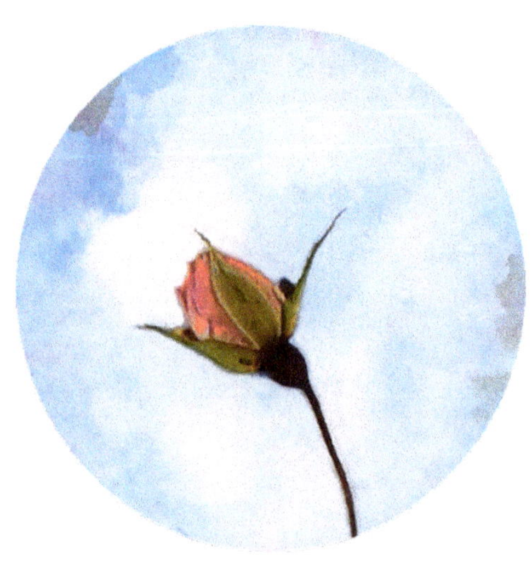

Step By Step,
Moment By Moment
A Technique From All My Guides
June 19, 2000

Here is a universal message for any of us who have a desire for abundance and success—the question of how to let it flow is probably one of my most often asked questions. I even got an answer when I dreamed one night that I was playing basketball with former quarterback Joe Montana (four time Super Bowl Champion.) In the dream, he told me that success came from "consistent effort toward a goal." The following message from my guides showed me their eternal patience. If they were willing to help me "moment by moment," then I needn't be afraid they might throw up their hands and give up on me. They were with me for the long haul, and I needed to learn that!

Dear One,

Open up to it. It is yours for the asking, and we are here and near for the help you need to create it—should you need us. Go forward—the world is yours. Work with the energy. Work with the love. Learn to create in this way. Step by step, inch by inch, take yourself where you want to go. You are here to learn to create and then open the path for others to do so as well. And, all will be well. We are with you. Call on us moment by moment if need be. We want you to learn this and will do all that we can to help you. Let us begin together—hand in hand, step by step, moment by moment. And it is one step at a time. That is how anything works. Desire, imagination and action. We're getting down to the nitty gritty now, so let us begin.

We await your call
in love and desire,
All your Guides

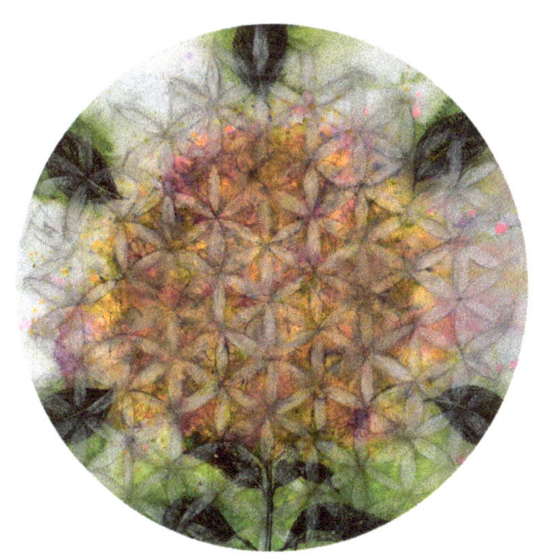

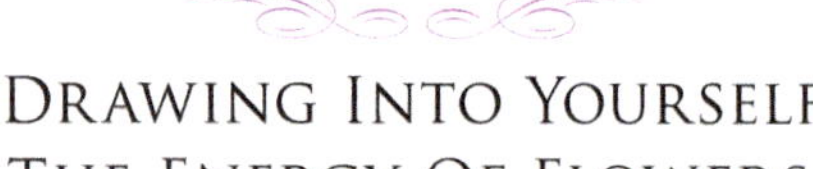

DRAWING INTO YOURSELF THE ENERGY OF FLOWERS
A TECHNIQUE FROM
WHITE EAGLE & WHITE DOVE
FEBRUARY 5, 1988

I received this beautiful technique long ago and forgot I had it. It was fun to find it again and realize that on some level I'd been using it for years. This message was an answer to an inquiry I had after having dreams of my female and male energies warring at night. In one dream I lined my cyclamen plants up in battle formation! From this message I wanted to know how to access female energy and then how to balance male and female energies. This is a wonderful message for all of us to understand the importance of being with flowers.

Paint flowers. Look at flowers. Understand flowers. In doing these things you will come to know and understand female energy. Flowers are so beautiful as they are—and they are just that, simply being who they are—not doing anything. And they are simply accepted for what they are—beautiful, flowing flowers. That's all. No more. They have nothing else to do but to be what they are. Nothing else is expected of them and they expect nothing else from themselves.

Take a lesson from the flowers. Work with them in your garden and attempt to understand the deeper meaning/energy of who they are. Bring this energy into your own life. Let it flow within yourself. Learn to flow with the energy of God. Let that soft, beautiful energy into your life and into your heart and it will unleash that same soft and flowing energy that sleeps inside of you.

Painting flowers has helped you get closer to this energy and understand it. It is for a reason.

You want this energy. By getting in and painting flowers, and understanding them as deeply as you need to in order to paint them, you will draw this feminine energy into yourself. Decide to be a flower and act it out. On retiring at night draw into yourself the energy of flowers for you to sleep with all night. This will help you soften and open up to this energy to balance out your energies. You will then realize the benefit of this energy, how good the softness feels, and that it is not to be feared. Enjoy both energies. You have tended to fear the feminine energy and the vulnerability, and have preferred the masculine energies thinking they would take you further and protect you more. What is really the truth is that the balance will set you free—with no boundaries and no place to go than "to be." Welcome to the serenity of being-ness.

White Eagle & White Dove

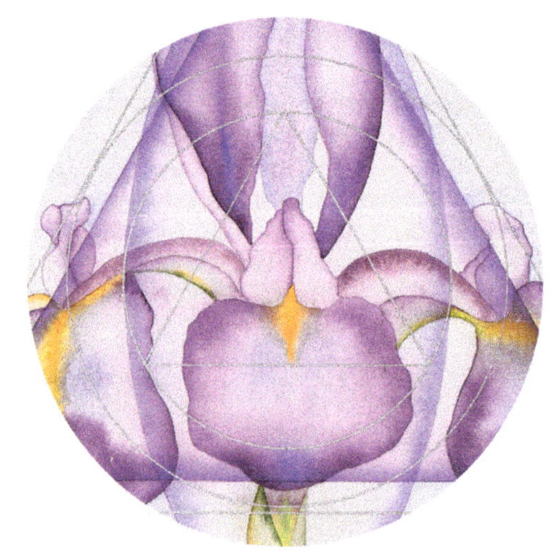

STEPPING CLOSER TO THE LIGHT
A TECHNIQUE FROM WHITE EAGLE
FEBRUARY 2, 1988

Messages from White Eagle are so simple and loving. This came to me when I was sick and had asked for help. I'd received White Eagle's assistance about six months earlier, although I didn't know it was him. He had come as I was falling asleep one night, in response to a request I'd made for a healing to prevent a tooth from dying. He appeared to me in my half-dream state as a Medicine Man, all in white feathers and white leather. Two nights in a row he danced a Medicine Dance around me and on the second night my body released the disease with a groan and powerful gush of air from my mouth. Later in disbelief, the endodontist searched but could find no sign of the original problem, and I left his office without the scheduled root canal. So this time when I saw the Medicine Man, again as I drifted asleep, I asked if he was the White Feathered Medicine Man who had helped with my tooth.

That is just one of many images that I have. It is used when I am doing healing and it is not shown much to others. We again are most pleased and honored to enter into your aura and bring assistance. It is also good that you have called on us. Do not be shy, and release your feelings of unworthiness. This merely causes blockage, and a true healing and cleansing can not be complete if you cling to unworthiness. You are most worthy or we would not be here. We are so pleased you are receptive to us and we go where there is receptivity. We are here to help. Ask for help. This is not a lessening of your strength, nor a weakness, for you know where your true strength is and you are reaching for it. It is in this partnership of you and God that your true strength lies.

Let go of being ill. Decide to get better. Want to get better and do not continue to cling to the old. Do not fear moving along. Decide to move forward. Ask for help in moving forward. That's all. It's really quite simple. It's a choice and all that is required of you is to make it. Make the choice. And if it is a choice to take another step closer to the light, we are right here at your elbow, assisting you so you won't fall, giving you strength and encouragement and support and cheering you on. Also smiling and waiting and watching for your next experience of joy—which is a promise. Is this so hard, really? Funny, how we have to learn to choose and enjoy joy. Be that as it may—we encourage you to make that choice knowing we are right here with you.

So, how do you let go? Tonight, as you retire, call on us to be with you and assist you in taking your next step—thus letting go of the previous one. That's all. We welcome you to your next level with open arms, open hearts and deep, deep love. And we do love you so. Bless you, and remember we are always near.

White Eagle

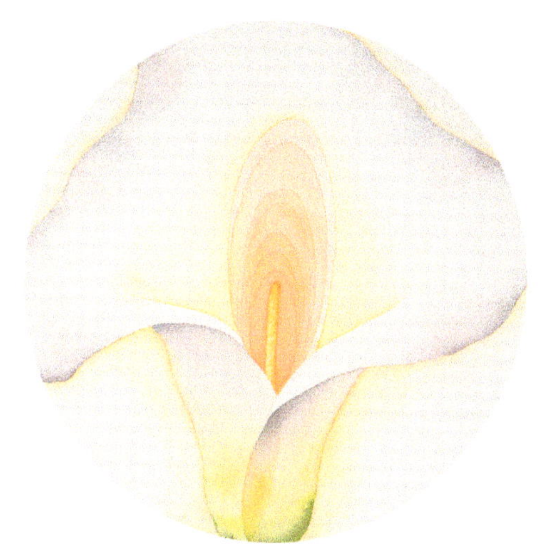

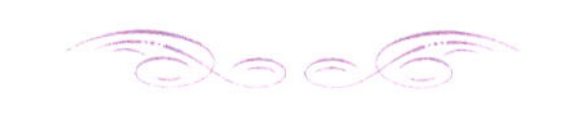

Creating Your Own Reality With Love

Learning to create my reality with love has certainly been a lifelong core lesson for me and maybe it is for all of us. I have received many messages like this one telling me to take one step at a time and that I would be helped, "hand-in-hand" and "moment by moment." That speaks to me of my guides' eternal patience.

Dear One,

You've been wondering what's been going on and why you feel as if you are not moving ahead. Don't let appearances fool you. You are moving ahead quite nicely and have been learning a much needed lesson. Besides, you cannot move much further ahead now anyway until you learn this lesson. The lesson is about creating your own reality with love. It is about reaping the consequences of what you think and imagine. So, you can see, it's a big one. And it must be learned before you can reap the rewards that you so desire. You must think them into being. You must know they are there before they manifest. You must believe—and all will be yours. It's back to the drawing board if your thoughts and imagination can't wrap themselves around your success. There has been a clearing out of old patterns and old ways of thinking. It must be so. You have to be able to expand your mind to encompass all that you want and then open your arms and your heart to receive it. Without this, success is not possible. What do you say? You must learn the process of loving what you want into manifestation. You must learn the process of wanting things with love. And allowing them into your life. First, as thoughts and beliefs.

First, as possibilities. This is how you grow. By learning to stretch your love. First, for yourself. To give yourself all that you want and need IN LOVE!

We know it has been difficult for you in the past to open up to the realization that there are things you want. But, if you think about it, that's how you grow—by wanting things, going after them and embracing them into your life. Proving that you can do this is a great lesson to oneself—and you have done this before and know how to do it. Go deeper now. Explore the depth of yourself and what you desire—learn that you can accomplish and learn the power of creation and co-creation. Like you've read about Jesus, what he did was always with love. Can you do this? Can you find this in your heart to love yourself enough to give yourself what you want? Give yourself success—because this is something you want so much. You want to prove to yourself that you simply can succeed! Go—Succeed! Do it by steps and then each small step will be an accomplishment and a success! You have never really taken good enough care of yourself. It is time now to do so—and we are with you to help. Begin a program of creating success by creating what you want for yourself.

Obviously this has to start with you becoming aware of what your desires are!

We know you want clothes.

OK!

We know you want to travel.

OK!

We know you want to get your artwork out to the world.

OK!

Admit it, own it, go for it!

The world can be yours.

It is for the asking!

Can you believe that? That is your lesson now. This is what you must learn and embrace.

It's really about expanding consciousness. The more you want and the more you can imagine, the more that will be yours. It's all light anyway. Expand your light! Don't hold it back. Learn to accept and enjoy. Learn to create and co-create. Learn that you are the All and therefore can have it all!! It's all about energy, creation, attention, intention. So where are your

energies,

creations,

attentions,

intentions,

and, where is your love?

You can have it all!

We are here and are always with you.

Just ask! Everyone!

STOP FOCUSING

ON WHAT

YOU

CAN'T HAVE

AND

START FOCUSING

ON

WHAT YOU

CAN HAVE

AND THAT

YOU CAN HAVE

IT ALL!

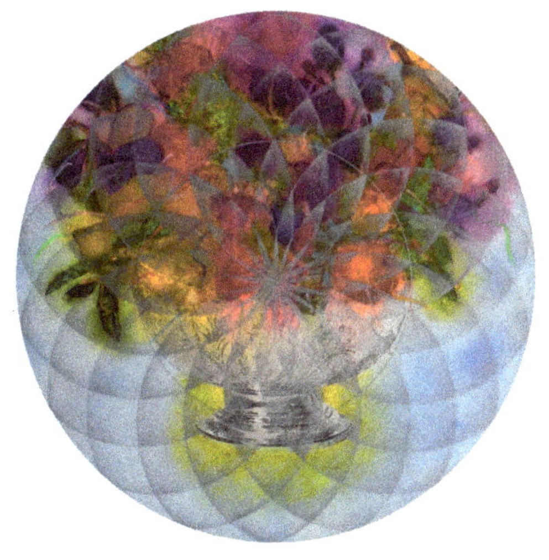

ASK AND YOU SHALL RECEIVE, ALL OF YOU ARE CONDUITS

A TECHNIQUE TO EVERYONE FROM ST. GERMAINE
DECEMBER 15, 2000

St. Germaine speaks to me and to all of us with this message. His playfulness and humor come through here and that tells me, "Don't take yourself so seriously!"

My Dear One,

OH—what you are learning! Continue—we are with you. And, as we remind you, always, stay open and connected to us for we are always here for your support, for your success and really the key to your life's work. Yes—us—your guides—are part of your chosen path, your right work and with whom you will succeed. Think on it. It will not happen otherwise. We are in this together and this is your work. Bring us forward, introduce us to others, help others grasp the endearing love we have for them and our enduring presence in their lives. We are here—we won't go away. We are here for a purpose and you are that purpose. Welcome to the Cabaret! You are in the process of understanding what you are here to do. We understand. And we push and prod you along. Yours is a most wonderful chosen path. You have chosen and you have been chosen. Sink into it. And, like we hear you saying—put on the magic shoes and go for it. Do not take them off—for the shoes fit and you are to wear them now. You have had trouble with your feet—well, actually, you've had trouble with finding shoes that are right for you. You now know that what you need are the Magic Shoes which have been waiting for you to put on. Yes, a little like Cinderella trying to recapture her magic slippers. Well, yours are at hand. We will help you put them on and give you permission to wear them. And, will you fly when they are on your feet, a perfect match, for a perfect life. Your life now is what you came to do. We are in this together. You receive the information we reveal to you and you bring it to the world. Like a conduit. Free flowing information from God. Actually available to anyone who wants to open up to themselves. All the information, available to everyone in this way. This is your message— our message. All of you are conduits—just open up and be filled. Keep the lines clear and open. Ask and you shall receive. Knock and the door will be opened. The I AM is within and can be heard by all.

"Well," I asked, "What do I do next?"

Go to the boss—every day. Check in. Ask what the plan is by going within and asking your guides, God, Goddess, All That is—Everybody. Ask everybody—what's up for today? We are all working together—so be part of the big plan and do your small part, for it will fit in the larger plan—which you may not know fully at the time. Just know that you are part of the plan— and when we all work together, each doing our small part—the whole will come together and purr like a well-oiled machine. It will work. And it will be a most wondrous on-going "play." So, step into your part and enjoy the performance. We are with you now and forever. You are never alone. Remember that. And join the play. Life is a Cabaret my friend!

Yours in Love Absolute,
absolutely!
St. Germaine and All

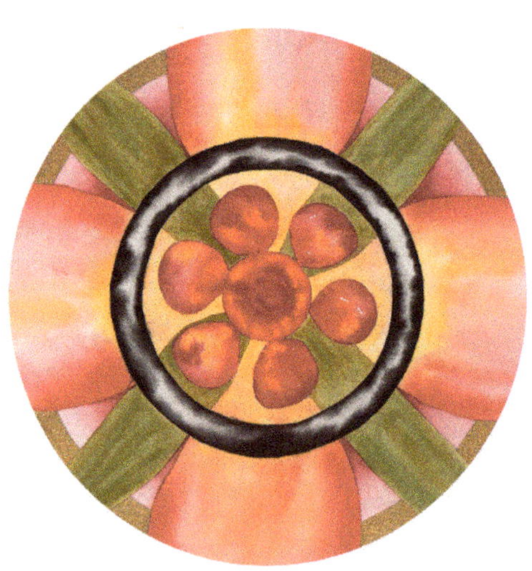

Using The Violet Transmuting Flame
A Technique From St. Germaine

Your work is our work and our work is your work. Remember that the colors are involved in this blessed work of ours—especially the purple transmuting flame. This is for everyone's use and we encourage your use of it and your communication to others of the wondrous results they may receive with their use of it. This is our job—the transmutation of the old, limited ways and beliefs so that the way may be cleared for the light and full potential of all that is.

I originally learned about the Violet Flame from my teacher Hope, in the meditation class I attended in the early 1970s. She presented weekly channeled messages and St. Germaine and the transmuting flame were often the subject. We were told that a greater gift for cleansing and rehabilitation had never been given, and that the principal color ray, or energies, on the planet at this time were the purple hues. I was later to learn that St. Germaine was my spirit guide and I did it by simply and ceremoniously asking who my spirit guide was. My dear friend, who had originally taken me to Hope's class, suggested I give it a try. "Just ask," she said.

After awaiting the allotted time after I'd asked—she said three days—I kept getting the name "Jerry." When I asked if he was the one, I was washed with violet light and the fragrance of violets. This was quite an experience, especially when others could smell the scent of violets around me and in my office—which lasted three days! It took me about a month to realize that "Jerry" was actually St. Germaine!

The Violet Light is used for cleansing, restoring and to bring peace and tranquility. St. Germaine called it the "cosmic eraser" in its ability to erase and "heal the wounds of error." The Violet Flame is also called the "freedom flame" as it releases past actions, and carries the qualities of freedom, joy, forgiveness and transmutation. St. Germaine is said to have had several incarnations on earth and, after he ascended, offered his gift of the Violet Flame to all who would invoke it with sincerity.

I have used the Violet Transmuting Flame many times through the years. I also call it the Purple Transmuting Flame. I use violet and purple interchangeably and I notice that St. Germaine does as well. I found that I was getting better results when I became more deeply focused, sincere, and said his decree out loud. When I use the Violet Transmuting Flame, this is what I do: I ask for help from God/Goddess, my High Self and St. Germaine, bring the issue I'm needing help with into my heart and visualize myself engulfed in the Violet Light. I have used this decree which was given by St. Germaine:

I blaze the Violet Fire from my heart consuming all that is not of the I AM.

I have used this on my morning walks and have found it to be very powerful. My experience has been that using the Violet Transmuting Flame is life changing. If you want to simplify this process you can do so by first acknowledging you have something inside which you want to heal or cleanse. Then bring the situation into your heart and ask for help from the Creator and your spirit guide as you use the Violet Light. It truly works wonders.

I have a brother-in-law who is really a man's man and isn't into any of this spiritual "stuff," or so I thought. One day he was wearing purple tennis shoes, and when I commented that I liked them, he told me his favorite color was purple!

It actually kind of surprised me and made me smile inside. I really like hearing that someone's favorite color is purple, and I seem to be hearing that more and more these days.

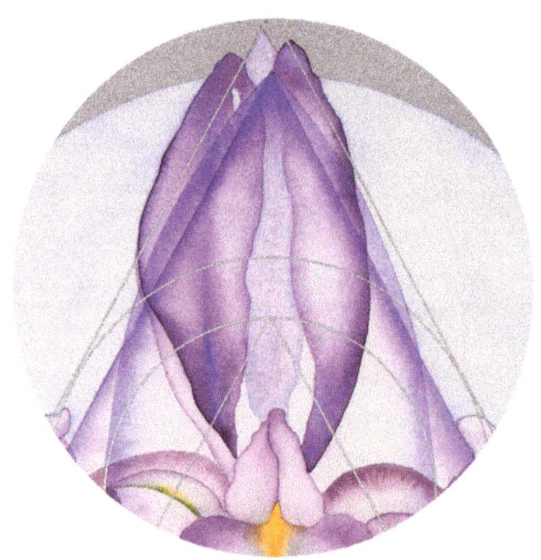

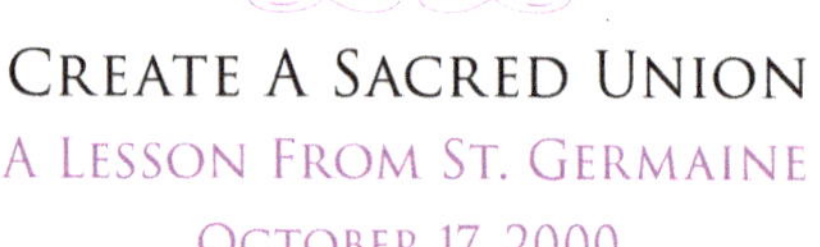

CREATE A SACRED UNION

A LESSON FROM ST. GERMAINE
OCTOBER 17, 2000

I got this message after I had a vision of complete peace and success as I surrendered and worked completely from my heart with St. Germaine. It was quite a profound feeling. I was moving ahead with my work, moving through the fear and excuses. I realized that a deeper relationship with spirit and a deeper trust of my own heart was what I needed. It's what we all need! I wrote, "What is the next step after this realization?"

Dear One,

Follow your heart—as always—for that is part of the learning and lesson—that you do what your heart desires. What is in your heart now? Have you checked? That is where you will find your true work and the fuel to sustain it. This is most important to realize. What is alive in your heart now? What is your heart wanting to express? What is your heart open to? What call is your heart responding to now? This is what you should ask yourself and respond to. This is what will, as always, give you direction. You will follow your heart and, as you do, show others how to do so as well.

We will be with you, standing beside you encouraging you all the way. It is our agreement and I am right next to you. We are brethren and united in our mission. It is an honor to work with you and now we may begin in a relationship not unlike holy matrimony—a sacred union which is committed to the betterment of each partner. Blessed is our union! For we are now one and committed to the same thing—the love and growth of each other.

In Love Absolute,
St. Germaine

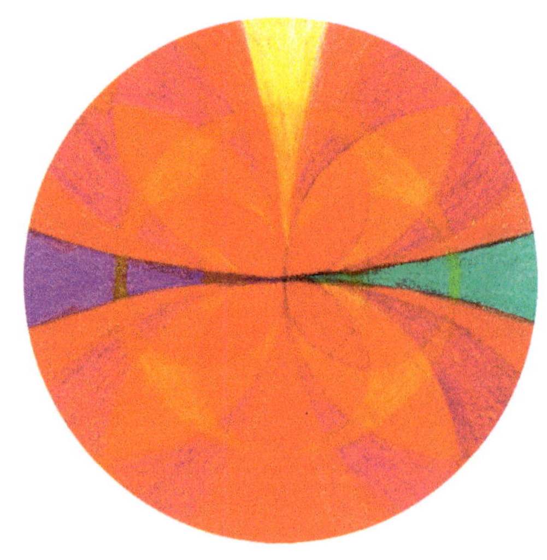

Use Color In Art To Receive Color's Gift
A Lesson From St. Francis
September 2, 1988

This is a wonderful message for us all, about color, the heart and art. In the fall of 1998 I decided to teach a class on color, after being urged to do so by my guides for a long time, and knowing that I would learn much myself. I asked St. Francis, whose presence I was feeling around the class, if he was actually going to be guiding it? I also inquired if it would be okay to reveal his influence, and was color really what the class was going to be about?

Color is a wonderful place to start, for what we are really doing here is opening and healing the heart. Making the heart feel more comfortable about opening wider for oneself, and then in the future to work with others from a place of love. Using paint to focus the mind on color is a great way of entering into the realm of the divine. For color truly is a gift, and in this way, using color in art, you can more deeply receive the gifts color has for you. This can be a most beautiful experience both from within and without. Start with the focus and intention of opening your heart to color and learn how to receive and perceive the effects of color on yourself. Practice opening to the subtleties, for the depths of color are received and perceived on energy levels you may still be new to. This is a grand adventure. Simply start with a desire to open your heart and receive what is around you and for you. I think you will be happily surprised and amazed. And we wish you great love and joy as you venture into this realm. You ask—will I be guiding you? I will be near always, but let color be your guide. My only request is that you remember to listen to the guidance and trust it. This is also part of the lesson and the gift.

We bless you with deep love,
St. Francis

And, as for you Michele, be a good example and show others and share with others the profound effect color has had on your life. That is the lesson for you and the gift!

"The title then (of the class?)" I asked.

"Open Your Heart to the Gift of Autumn Color."

I taught the class at Land of Medicine Buddha, a Buddhist retreat center in the Santa Cruz Mountains, and let everyone know that it was being inspired by St. Francis. No one flinched. We explored seven colors in seven evenings, one each week, starting with red and ending with violet. Our medium was watercolor and our format was mandalas, which is what I'd been teaching for years. The idea was to look at and deeply see the autumn colors around us and receive their gifts. It was a special class and very powerful. I felt it was a coming out for me as I began painting bigger paintings on full-sized sheets of paper, and started sharing the messages about color I had been receiving. I taught the class again the following spring focusing on the gift of spring colors. I taught it through community education and called it "Mandala Color Healing." Some of the paintings included in this book were painted in those classes.

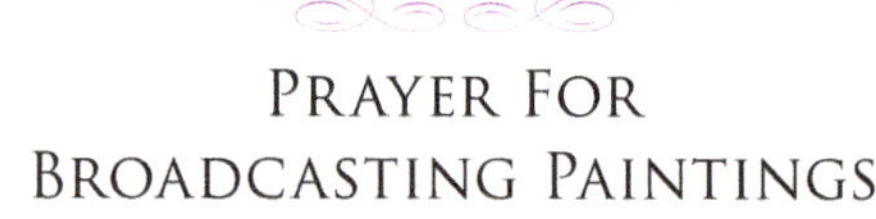

PRAYER FOR
BROADCASTING PAINTINGS
A TECHNIQUE FROM ST. GERMAINE

I have often used my paintings as tools to help others connect with spirit through the essence of a painting. I do this by broadcasting a painting (visualizing the sending of it,) which I've selected intuitively, and imagining its energy going to a recipient, or even to myself. You can try this yourself by first simply declaring the intention of receiving energy from a painting. Then either lay your hands on, or put your name on a piece of paper and put it on the painting, along with this prayer of intention from St. Germaine. Sit back and relax. It's a good idea to give yourself a space of about thirty minutes of quiet to do this process. Know that you may feel something, or you may not, or maybe you'll get an insight at a later time. It's different for everyone and different every time you do it. This can be done with any of the paintings in this book.

(Person's Name)
May the spirit of our blessed Creator
nurture, nourish and bless you
in your spiritual journey.
May your heart be opened
to receive this grand love
so that you will never again forget
your connection to it,
and know that it is,
and always has been,
within you.
May you know this love completely.
May this love make you whole.

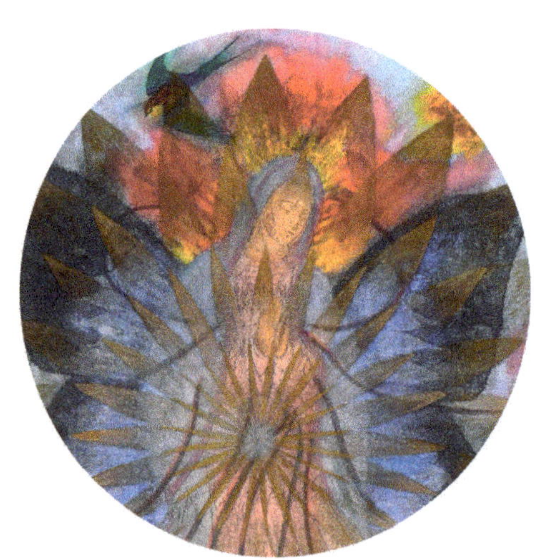

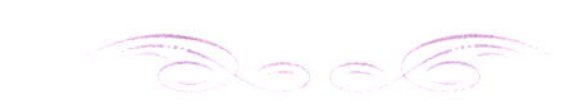

Heal Yourself With Color
A Technique From St. Germaine
January 2, 1997

Heal yourself with color. You can do it. Go outside and bathe in the colors of nature. Breathe them in. Activate your spine—the energies therein. By color. Open up to it. You can do it. Choose light over the darkness and the negative way. This will heal you. Go out into nature. Bring your writing book. See what color calls to you and write down what it says to you and do what it tells you to do.

Yes, you do need to be outside. The powerful energies of color are felt through the use of sun energy being reflected off of objects, especially nature. The colors will heal you and align you. Keep experiencing them and allow the work on you to be done. And, the learning and remembering. Color is a most powerful healer and you want to learn this. Here it comes. Be trusting. Be open. When you experience it, you will be most surprised. And then you will desire to keep yourself immersed in color. Keep in color and out of your negative thoughts and your wandering mind. This is one of the values of your painting. Keeping alive and aligned with color. Color is at your fingertips and is one of the most powerful tools given to man. You will remember this and help others with it. What a joy. What beauty. Color could be used far far more than it is, and now it is hardly used at all! This means a slowing down, a complete change in the way people live in their world, and in their life, with nature. This will be a complete healing.

We are grateful for your attention
to this most magnificent endeavor
and we look forward to working with you,
St. Germaine

This message is really key to this book. After receiving it I ventured out to the ocean bluff near my home, sat on a bench surrounded by green grass and tried to attune myself to green. Nothing happened right away and I felt bad because I didn't think I could do it. This is actually not unusual for me when facing a new challenge. I want to—and think I should be able to—succeed immediately. Then I saw a big weed and thought, "That's me today, nothing special, just a plain old weed!" But I felt God loved me and the weed just as we were. We didn't have to be anything else other than the best we could be that day. I didn't have to come up with some great, profound spiritual revelation. Allowing myself to be small, with just the hope of evolving beyond it, gave me permission to relax and my first color poem came, "Be Green, Green Said." This poem is in Part II, page 39, "Flower Energy Paintings: The Colors and Their Messages." I hope this is helpful when you go to try this technique.

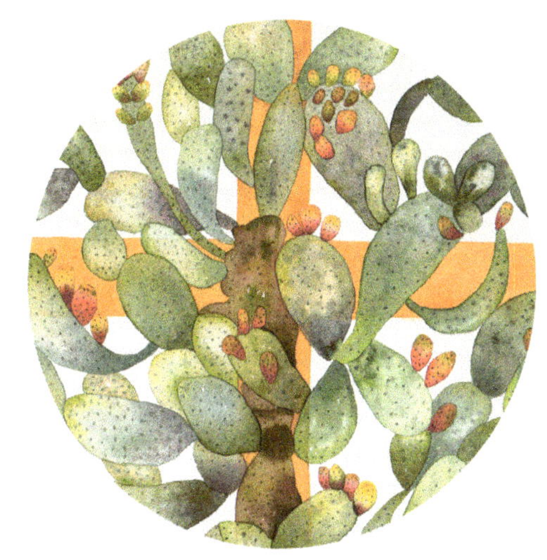

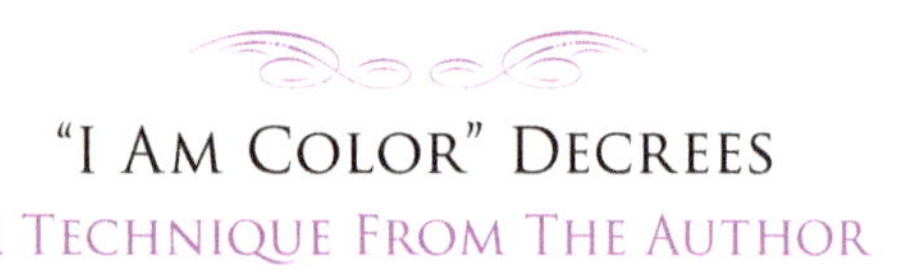

"I Am Color" Decrees

During one morning meditation, I spontaneously started saying these declarations of color. I found it so energizing and joyful and was really rather amazed at how great I felt. When you try it, speak out loud so that your biology hears it. Feel yourself as the color as you breathe it into your entire body. Enjoy!

I am all light,
I am all color.
I am red,
I am orange,
I am yellow,
I am green,
I am blue,
I am indigo,
I am violet.
I am all the blendings I need.
I am peace, I am love,
I am spirit, I am power,
I am life,
I am the Glow of God.

Now try decreeing that you are pastel colors—which are made by adding white or light to the original colors. It gives this a different kind of feeling within. To me it seems so soft.

I am pink,
I am tangerine orange,
I am lemon yellow,
I am lime green,
I am powder blue,
I am periwinkle,
I am lavender!

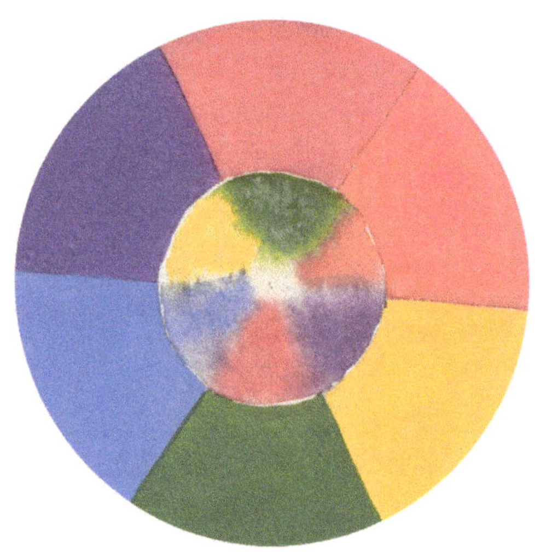

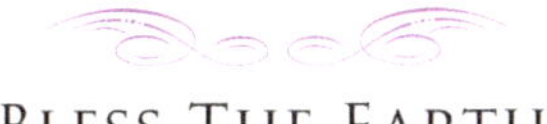

BLESS THE EARTH,
BLESS THE FLOWERS
A REQUEST FROM CHIEF SEATTLE
FEBRUARY 19, 2001

Chief Seattle came to me in a dream as a magenta and golden yellow flower. I asked him for a message on awakening. This, I believe, is directed to us all.

On my morning walks, and after I give thanks for my own flowers, I enjoy appreciating the flowers in my neighbor's gardens. I surround myself with flowers throughout my day. Once, in-between jobs, I had a temporary assignment at a corporation in Silicon Valley which made military equipment (sometimes I couldn't believe where I'd find myself!) I survived each day by breathing in the beauty and the fragrance of the roses an elderly English engineer would bring me from his garden. Flowers feed me and my day is not complete without them.

One morning, I noticed I was getting little electrical jolts when I looked at flowers. What an experience. As I looked more deeply at them, trying to understand what was happening, I could see, on a subtle energy level, geometrical patterns out of which the flowers were physically taking shape. I felt the electrical impulses in my heart and got very emotional. I realized the flowers were creating impulses to open my heart and what I was feeling was deep love. It was wonderful and I felt I had just glimpsed another level of reality.

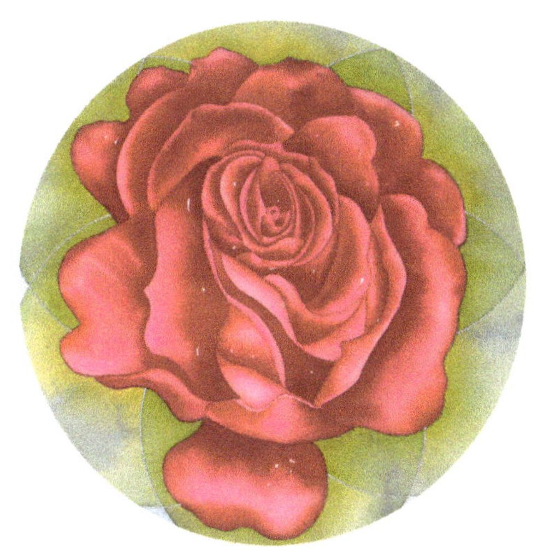

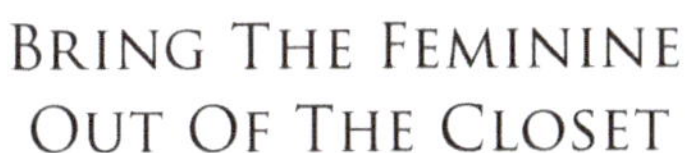

BRING THE FEMININE
OUT OF THE CLOSET
A SUGGESTION FROM THE MASTER
GUIDE GROUP AND ST. GERMAINE
OCTOBER 19, 2000

Whether male or female, this is a message for everyone. When I got it I was still in awe from the message I'd received from St. Germaine just two days before, "Create A Sacred Union." Union on this level with one's guides is a big step—at least it was for me. However, it seems to be a necessary one for what follows.

Dear One,

Yes we did get your attention, and know what is bubbling inside of you and has been doing so since our last communication. You are going deeper and it is real—you can feel it. You must enter into these areas which have previously been shut down, shut off and taken out of view. You are simply reaching a new level, and you know that that never stops. It sent shock waves through you and for this we are pleased. Another layer within is awakening and opening up. You can feel that it needs to, can't you? You are surprised that there is such a large area inside you that is still unexplored. This opening and realization is such good news. It must now be explored and you have been getting hints of this recently. You want to know what is next for you. Well this is it. Exploring that darkness within that has not been plumbed. Are you ready? It is about the feminine within—the Goddess energy—and you have been reluctant to look at it. But it is time now, for there is a wealth of information, energy and love here. Go in. You will see and utterly amaze yourself. You've been skirting it for too long and now is the time. I think you are ready. You are surprised to hear the Source is feminine and we will show you how to connect with it, for we know you are afraid. You are fearful for many reasons, as your lifetimes have not had a preponderance of positive female energy. You are to discover that now—or rediscover it, for you actually do know it from other realms. It's time to bring it through—and this has been your commitment in this incarnation from the beginning. To be so full of male energy and prefer it and then to learn of and balance with the female. You have much to remember! And, you will do it as you so desire—for you will realize the energy, love and power in it. It is most wondrous for you, as it will be for the whole world, to discover.

We know you have had a resistance to this and we acknowledge that and your fear—but it is time to move through that now and on to your commitment and to the job ahead of you. Interesting isn't it? Surprising, too.

And, you have been wondering about the name St. Germaine—received as you have done with the extra "e." This is correct for we are much larger than you can conceive, there are many more parts to us than you know, and the piece that is here with you has more feminine energy for good reason. It is the help you need for your assignment which is our assignment. We are bringing the feminine out of the closet and this kind of energy is needed and most beneficial for the job at hand. We will first be coaching the feminine energy out of you, balancing your energies, and then will take it out to the world. In otherwords, show others just how you did it. We have much work to do—let us begin!

What will our first assignment be as we continue to move out of the closet? How about calling on Mother Goddess to help—and ask for a sign. This can be fun—so let it be.

We bless you and keep you in our care.
We are always with you. So let us begin.
Your Master Guide Group
with the love light of St. Germaine

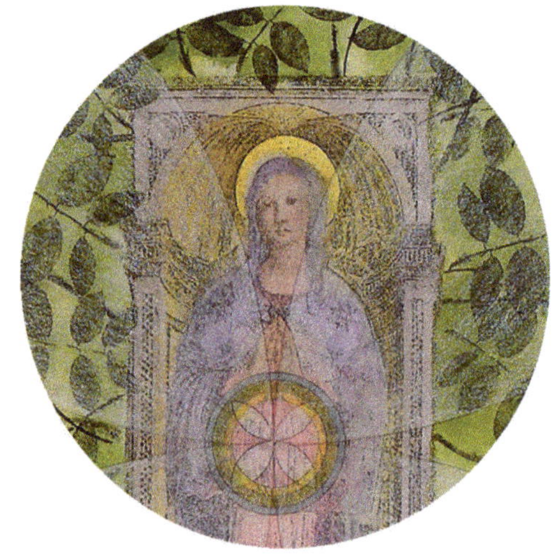

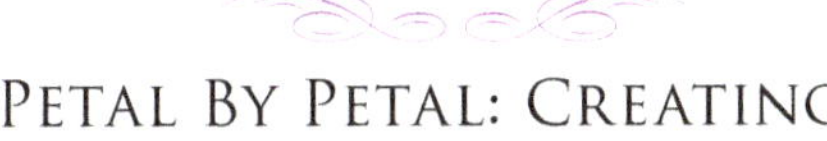

Petal By Petal: Creating A Color Wheel

As we come to the end of Part IV, it would not be complete without at least a few suggestions on how to create mandalas, which, I believe, are one of the greatest tools for opening the heart we have. In class I always start with color wheels to break the ice, so here are some pointers. Creating your own color wheel is a fun way to begin working with paint (or any other medium,) to learn about color and just plain get started. You can begin with the standard color wheel and get creative from there. The basic six-color wheel is made with a compass from a circle divided equally into six parts.

Try this: draw a circle with a compass. Call this circle A. Without moving the degrees of the compass, and using the same radius as circle A, go to the circumference (outside edge) of the circle and place the compass point anywhere on the line of the drawn circle. Wherever the pencil crosses the line of circle A make a tick mark. Place the compass point on that tick mark and repeat the process, making another tick mark where the pencil crosses circle A again. Go around the circle until you have six tick marks. Connect the tick marks opposite each other on the circle with a ruler. This gives you a circle like a pie, divided into six equal pieces.

Paint (or color in some way) the colors in order (red, orange, yellow, green, blue, violet) starting with whichever pie piece you'd like. It doesn't matter where you start, but once you begin, you need to put the colors in order. This is described with illustrations in my first book *Art in My Heart; The Power of Watercolor Mandala Making*. Also on my website, there is a sample chapter "Creating a Color Wheel," which can be downloaded for free: http://www.michelefaia.com/books/.

The fun part of this is to get creative with the design of the color wheel. Really, the sky's the limit. Divide a circle any way you like, yes, any way, and have fun! Add anything else to it you'd like; flowers, leaves, feathers, other designs. And, they <u>are</u> mandalas—circular, with a center, and symmetrical.

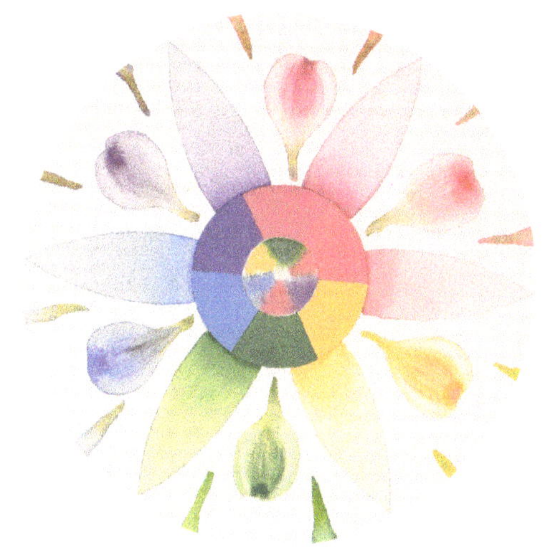

Making Mandalas: A Place To Start

Following the color wheel, where you can get comfortable with tools and color, here are some tips for getting started creating simple mandalas, should you want to give that a try. This is a simple way to begin and it's how I taught myself. You can do this with any medium: crayons, markers, chalk, pencils or watercolor, whatever feels the best to you.

I first began painting sacred circles, or mandalas, in 1992, drawn to them for reasons I was not completely sure of at the time. But I couldn't let go of the need to paint circles and quickly found them creating such peace, balance and healing in my life. I began to teach mandala making, teaching what I had learned simply through my own experience. "Start in the center and work out," I would say to my students, and I began mine in the same way. "Paint what's in your own center and let it develop from there." It was not unusual for me to see or feel a red dot at my center, so I'd begin my mandalas with that, and at that time red became commonplace at the center of my work. I didn't really know what it meant, it was a beginning, a place to start. Years later someone suggested that perhaps the red circle in my mandalas was a *bindi*, like the mark worn on the forehead of some Eastern Indian people. The *bindi* symbolizes the "all-point," a place from which everything rises and into which everything returns. In a mandala the *bindi* can represent the Oneness of all creation, the spiritual seeker's own center and the coming together of the two. I kind of like those explanations that are after-the-fact. And so the beginning for me was often red, as in *Shakti* in Part I, page 20. But it can be any color or any thing. A dot of color is just an easy way to begin if you feel unsure about where or how to start. From that dot, or center, work out from there, concentric layer by concentric layer. You may also, and I recommend it, write on the back of your paper an intention for the mandala. For example, you can begin it by writing, "I intend to co-create with spirit..." which will center you and connect you with spirit or the higher energies. If you need further guidance to get started on a mandala, one of the first assignments I give which is simple and fun to do, is to envision yourself as a flower. You can write on the back of the paper "Myself as a flower," or write it in your own words. Remember the mandala in Part III, page 54, where I wrote as an intention: "Myself as a flower, having fun,

loosening up?" Actually, you can have whatever intention you wish for your mandala, but having an intention really helps get the creative juices focused and flowing. It can even be "I'm open to whatever comes." As you work outward from the center, look into your own center or heart, and put down a representation of what's there. Usually this is done symmetrically, however it doesn't have to be symmetrical. It can be loosely circular, or it can be done within a circle, and I have done it both ways—whatever has been my mood at the time. The important thing is to trust yourself, let go of the fear of making mistakes, because there are none, and begin. And, remember always, have fun! When the mandala is finished, at the least, date it, and if you feel so inclined, give it a title, writing that on the back. I always do, or try to. It's a form of completion as well as a record of what was happening for that day. I really miss it if I haven't written a title or any notes (also valuable and important) on the back of a completed mandala, and my students have found it to be true for them as well.

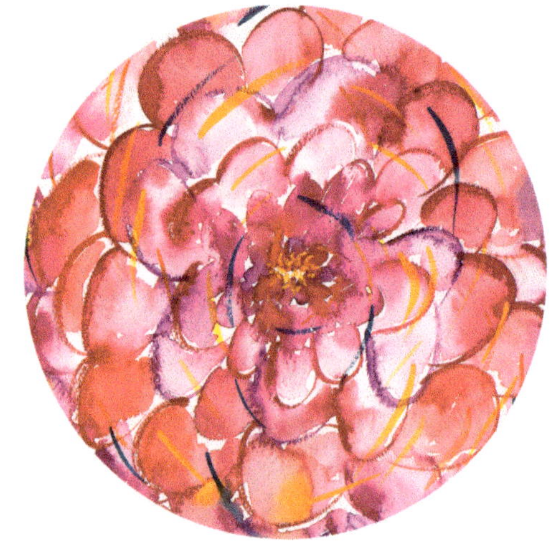

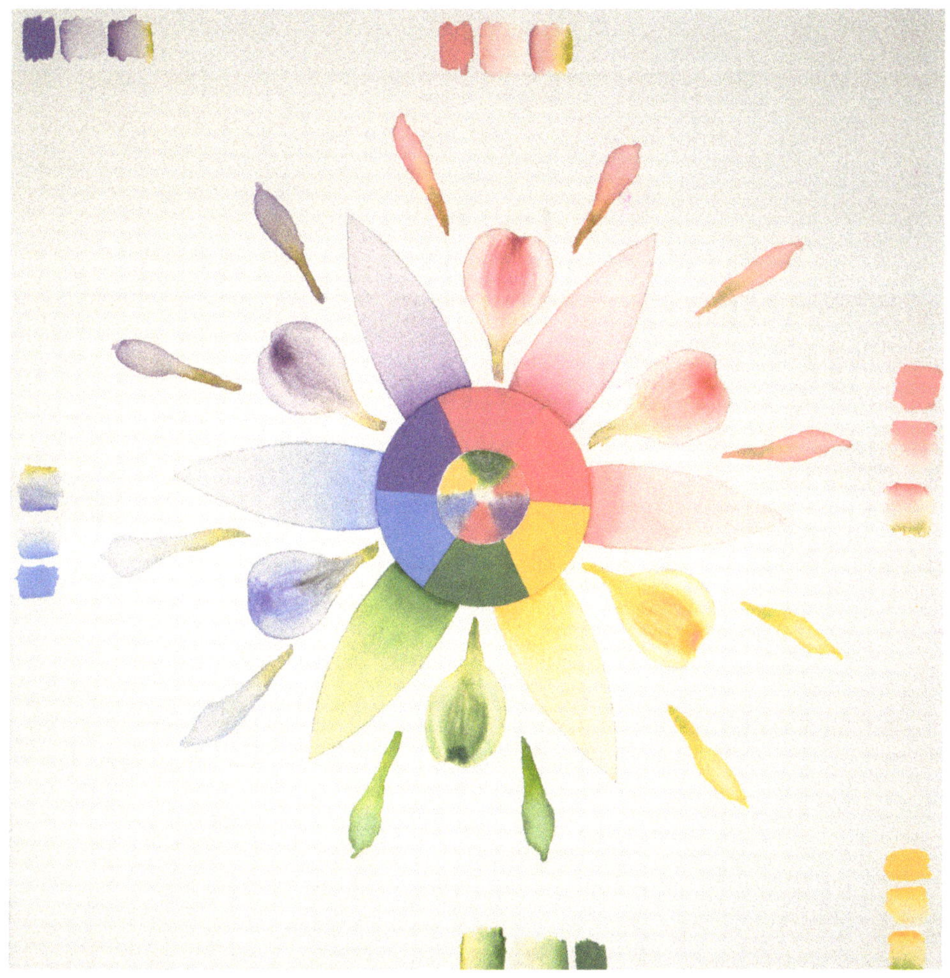

"PASTEL COLOR WHEEL"

Watercolor, 15" x 15" 1995

This color wheel was painted in a spring flower mandala class. The colors are all pastel, made by mixing each color with white. Petals in different colors float around the color wheel. I started many years ago to teach myself how to paint flowers. I had to. Flower painting was not taught in the schools I attended. I started by painting one petal of a flower at a time. I looked and looked at the petal with all its nuances before I began. I first got to know the flower, petal by petal. It seemed a lot less overwhelming to me that way. I learned my own techniques for attaining the effects I wanted by trial and error, and a lot of observing. Color wheels like this offer us a chance to practice techniques. And, any of us can use that. They are really wonderful practicing tools. When I start, I ask myself, "How can I entertain myself with this and what can I learn, or what do I want to learn this time?"

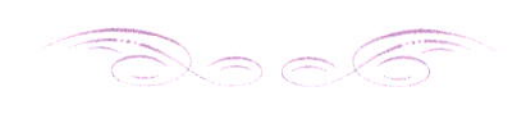

Enjoy Your Work And Your Calling
A Message And Assistance From The Collective Force Of Spirit
January 25, 1988

This message was originally directed to a group of lovely, colorful women with whom I had the pleasure of studying for a time. (Our teacher called us "Spectrum.") I know now that it was directed to the larger group who have found their way to reading this book. It serves as a perfect final message, wishing us all well as we begin our future work together.

Congratulations on following your hearts and your higher guidance. You have listened. Good.

You have much profound and far reaching work to do. You could not have been chosen.

With your own individual initiations you are all now ready to move outward and onward and accomplish the work you all agreed to do.

Congratulations for taking up your call. We will always be with you to assist you as needed, so do call. But you also have each other and a most powerful group you are. Call on each other, assist each other for you are all in it together. Most of all love and enjoy your work/your calling for it is a most beautiful gift which you have truly given yourselves. We send our love and blessings and are so happy that you have joined our work from the unseen. We welcome you. Blessings and joy to you as you begin your work—as we begin our work—together.

The Collective Force of the Spirit

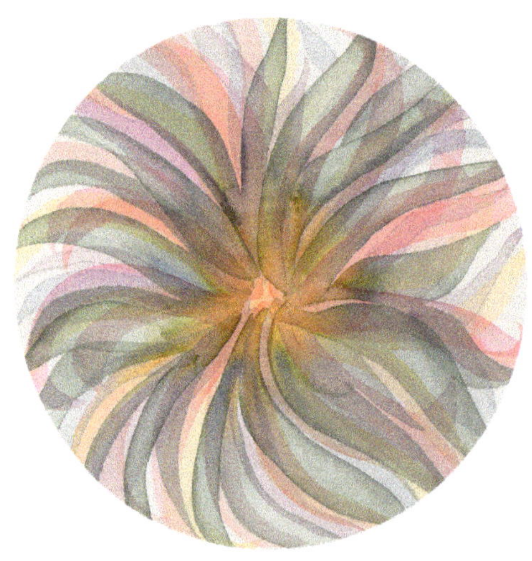

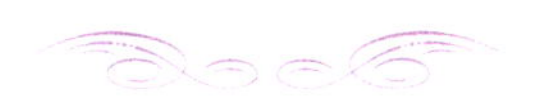

Conclusion (To Parts I-Iv)
A Message And Suggestion From St. Germaine, St. Francis & The All

The following is the message I received when I asked my guides if they had any words for the conclusion, or what I thought was to be the conclusion. It's interesting that they say that the work is "complete for the moment," which for a very long time totally escaped me because the book <u>wasn't</u> finished yet. The message is addressed to both myself and the reader.

Our work together now is complete for the moment on these most powerful tools, light and color. We commend your adherence to the program at hand and your dedication to this project and the process, both internally and externally, which it took to complete the work. We thank you. As well, we thank those who have followed this journey, along with your own personal one, and have come to know what this work has asked of you.

The journey for the author began with doors opening with the use of the violet color and the recognition of her spirit guides. Her doorway "in" began with the iris and many more doors opened from there. Everyone has their own doorway inward, their own symbols and the help of many, many unseen helpers. The information presented here with these most powerful tools of light and color may be used by everyone. Some will work for some, and others will work for others. Use what you can because they have been given in love, and if they touch your heart, they can be most helpful and valuable. But this book is also to serve as an encouragement for everyone to find their own doorways in, contact their spirit guides and ask for and receive tools that are specific to them. There is not one of you that cannot do the same thing this author has done and we strongly encourage you to do so.

We are most pleased to have touched you, as you have touched us. And, yes, that is true.

We send you
our deepest love and blessings,
St. Germaine, St. Francis

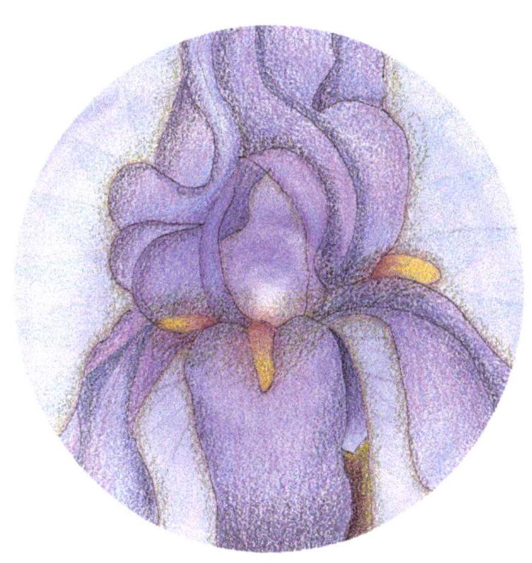

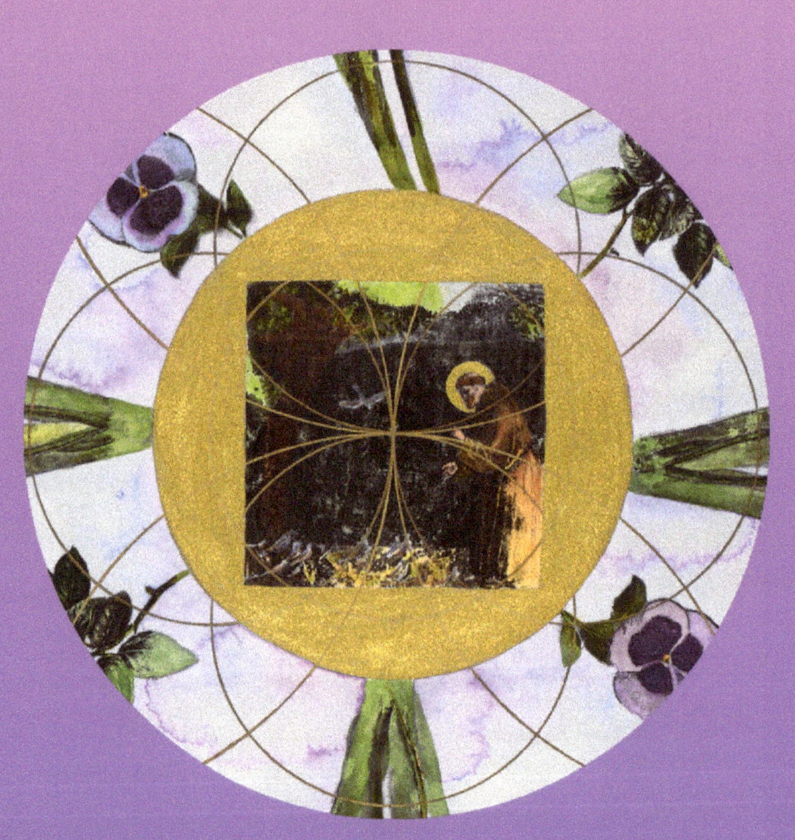

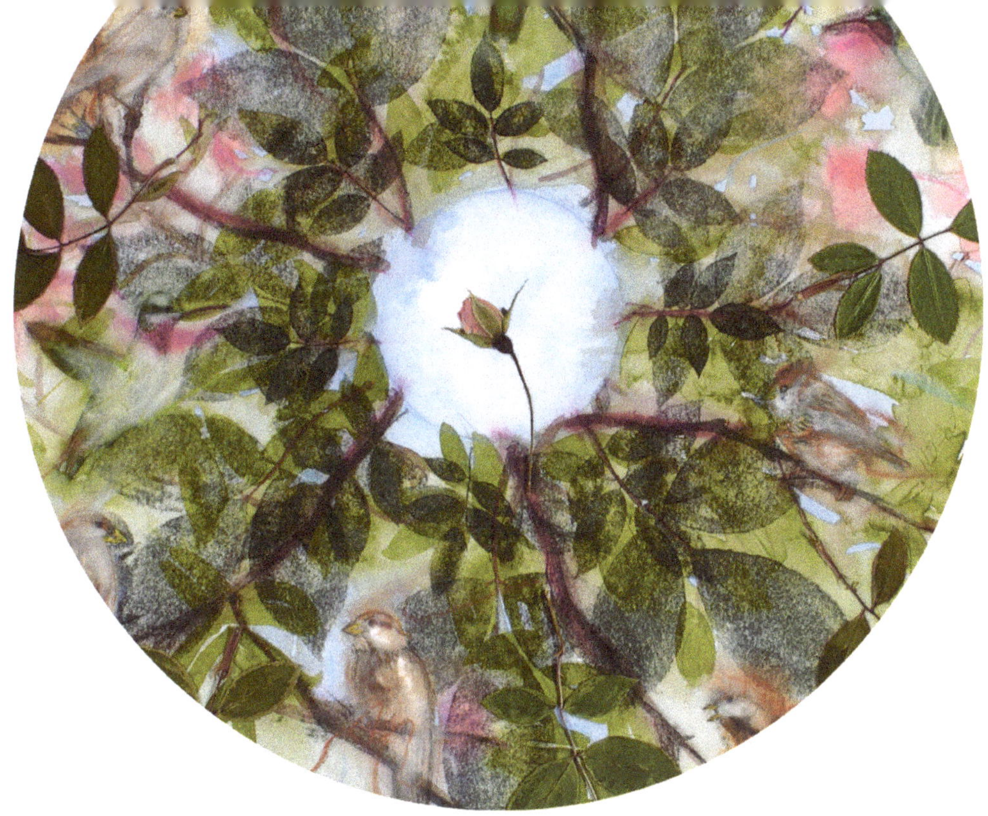

PART V

TAKING IT TO HEART

I really did think that this book was finished at the Conclusion of Part IV. Originally I had transcribed the whole book, what turned out to be Part I-IV, and had professional photography done of my mandalas. Then I put it on the shelf waiting for the next step. That turned out to be a breast biopsy, which was positive, and I was diagnosed with cancer.

I stopped teaching and painting, and didn't start painting again for about two years, somehow convinced I'd lost my ability and my creative spark. As spiritually tuned in as I thought I was, I was very confused as to how this turn of events had happened. I withdrew from everyone. I think I was feeling shame about getting cancer too. It was a very dark time for sure. When I did begin to paint again, I felt like I was painting myself out of a hole. I painted every day, feverishly, as I tried to push through the tremendous anxiety. I connected with old, stuffed emotions, deep grief and so many, many tears brought up by the encounter with cancer. I was raw. I saw a psychotherapist who helped me with connecting to and healing my emotions.

"Cancer saved your life," she said. "If you would have kept stuffing your emotions, they would have killed you."

I honestly didn't know I was doing that. I thought my stiff-upper-lip attitude and holding in my feelings since I was a child, was admirable. But it was just making me ill. As I painted and healed, grief and many other hidden emotions surfaced. I cried through the emotions, and all the while I was seeing visions of flowers and nature, which I then painted into mandalas. What the visions meant I did not know, other than I figured they had something to do with my healing. So, I just kept going and kept painting. The visions were full of incredibly bright lights, color and moving geometry. They were really something. I saw mostly flowers which were innumerable. I was flooded with amaryllis, fuchsias, poppies, camellias, irises, roses, orchids, hydrangeas, pansies, lilies, cyclamens, cosmos, primroses, lotuses, poinsettias and zinnias, to name a few! I would paint the mandala and, barely taking a breath, put that aside and start another painting. While I was painting I felt good and centered. I produced an amazing body of work, surprising even myself.

Eventually I got a part time job in an antique and garden shop, which had beautiful gardens and lots of flowers. It was good for my soul and got me out of the house and away from too much self-reflection. When I saw that the store sold a lot of art, I took a chance and started selling prints of my mandalas there, which was new for me. I found that I liked selling my work and did really well with it. Then I was asked to teach again. I promised myself I would only go back to teaching if I had fun and if everybody else did as well. It worked and I found I was enjoying myself!

It was then that I realized this book, now on the shelf for quite a number of years, needed an epilogue. That turned into Part V. I knew that it was to include some of my newest mandalas which I had done during my deeper healing. But I had painted so many of them! I decided several mandalas with their descriptions would be chosen along with a few channeled messages, making the format for Part V slightly different from Parts I-IV. Then, I noticed I was dragging my feet as I faced the fear of opening myself to the world. These new mandalas came from a very deep place and I had to wait until I was fully ready to share them.

Maggie, a friend who I had not seen in over a year after she had moved to the East Coast, "happened" to stop by my job.

"How's the next book coming?" she asked.

Seeing her was never a coincidence.

Her nudge got me going on my first book and now she was nudging me again, about this book.

Having delivered her message, my friend left, and of course I couldn't stop thinking about it. So I asked for a message and got this as I journaled:

Yea! Go for it! You are a writer and a beautiful one at that. Get to writing. You have much to say.

I wrote, "I don't know how to proceed. I need help and guidance."

You will be guided—each step. Take one step at a time. Be centered. Be connected.

I asked, "Is this about the Divine Feminine?"

Yes—and more. Open yourself fully to the information which will come through. And that will heal you also.

I wondered, "Are there more of my paintings to go in it?"

Yes, of course.

With excitement I proceeded. I did what I'd done with the first part of the book, I got out my pendulum and dowsed. Over the backs of a stack of paintings I asked whether this piece or that was to go into Book II. I made a "yes" pile and a "no" pile which was fun and entertaining. After the mandalas were chosen in this way, it was time to understand why they were chosen and write about them. This was, of course, a necessary part of my healing story. I would write about the chosen mandalas only after asking for and receiving a message from St. Germaine.

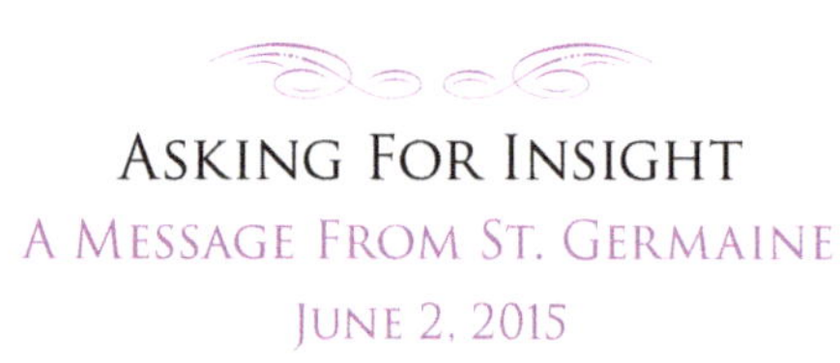

Asking For Insight

A Message From St. Germaine

June 2, 2015

As I was finishing the writing of Part V I tried to put it all together and make sense of my process. I sat down with my journal and asked St. Germaine for his insight. What he said touched me very deeply and I cried.

This is what I wrote: St. Germaine, I have never asked you about my journey through cancer. What is your take on it, especially with regard to the book?

Dear One,

We know it was a tough journey for you and it still holds an emotional charge.

We love you and care for you every day as we are asked and allowed to by you. Let us continue to help you through your continuing journey. We are never far—just a request away.

Yes, it was so hard and still makes me emotional when I think about it—so I don't always like thinking about it!

We are always here to assist. Don't be afraid to ask us for help. It will make your time through the pain and difficulty easier for you—and more understandable. We were with you through it all, and helped as we could. Remember, you didn't want any help and so our hands were tied to a degree. But we were beside you all the way.

Why was it so hard?

There was an opening that was happening within you and which you had asked for. You were holding on so tight to your old ways, that the cracking open was more difficult. We didn't like to see you in such pain, which really wasn't necessary. It came from your resistance and fear. We brought you flowers to help you make your way through the journey more pleasant, more bearable, more loving. Flowers are traditionally given as a gift of love from one to another in your world. We were giving you gifts to love you, so that you could know you were cared about. We gave them to you as visions and we saw that the flowers did help you. We were most pleased when we saw you respond to these gifts and paint them. It was all part of your growth in spirit, and you responded so beautifully. It made our hearts sing and we saw that the visions of flowers comforted you. As you were comforted, you opened your heart more and more. You grew in many ways. Eventually the pain lessened and your life smoothed out.

We know that for a long time it didn't occur to you to include these paintings, done through this difficult journey, in your/our book. It is good you listened from within and knew that some of them needed to be included so as to tell the fuller story. They are beautiful paintings and carry so much spirit in them and so much healing. You have always wondered how it was possible to have created such beauty while you were struggling so. The answer is that you were following spirit and your guidance and you were letting go to it, a little at a time. Yours was a most difficult journey and we commend you for staying on path. We do think you knew on some level that we were with you and that you were being guided. You trusted and that is beautiful. We hated to see your pain, but the path and destiny was something you wanted. You wanted to open your heart and release the past. We were helping you through your resistance and we all came through it. Stunning! Remarkable! Beautiful!

We take your hands in ours and tell you once again how much you are loved and cared for. Never alone, never far from you, we bless you dear one and thank you for this powerful, important and beautiful journey you have made.

In deepest Gratitude, Love and Respect,
We remain, St Germaine and All,
Your family in Spirit

Mandala One

ABOUT THE PAINTING

"Stand In Your Strength"

Watercolor and colored pencil, 7.5" x 7.5" c.1994

Create The Greatest Vision Of Yourself

The first painting selected for Part V is actually an energy symbol I created from images I received in two dreams. At the time I had just become a certified EMF Balancing Technique practitioner. My instructor and I were experimenting with creating mandala energy symbols for broadcasting healing energy. This is one I created from energy patterns in my dreams.

Stand in Your Strength was made by combining the imagery from the following two dreams.

The first dream was four circles which intersected and created a fifth circle in the center with a four-petaled pattern. The circles were colored light—the top circle was white, the circle on the bottom was red, green was to the right and the circle on the left was violet. I heard this message: *All things begin with this.*

Four months later I dreamed of another pattern of four, this time it was primarily red with a bit of various other colors in it. This dream came following two energy sessions I had done with clients. I had gotten a bad headache, was exhausted and realized I had taken on their energies. At first I thought the red pattern, which I called the four-petaled pattern, was an energy healing symbol for others. I asked in my journal what it was for and I got this message.

Take care of yourself first, my dear, and all else will take care of itself from there. You must get centered and aligned with your deep center. This is the lesson here—for you to once again see the necessity of taking care of yourself, and for being in the Now with your Self and with God.

The red painting of the petal formation you received in your dream is a grounding device for yourself first. Use it and understand it first in this capacity. Ground yourself in your own body, connect to the earth and your physicality—become strong through the work on yourself here. Be strong, plant two feet on the ground, stand firm in your own strength and do not let anyone knock you off your beam. It is your space, and your deep connection down into the earth and to this reality. You are here and you deserve to be here fully. In red you are strong and grounded, fully alive, fully awake and fully here. Your desire is to be fully awake to the life you are in here and now, and to fully participate in the energies of life—all life. Open up to it, embrace it, enjoy it, welcome the energy that you are in your life connection here. Appreciate the opportunity you have been given to open and grow and interact with all the energies around you. This will transform you. Be here in order to partake and participate in the fullness and glory of all the possibilities. This is truly creation—taking in energies, transforming them and returning the energies back into the flow of life. Be here, open, receive, grow, transform, radiate out the new creations from your stance in strength. This is the beginning of creativity—unique and strong within yourself to reach out and welcome energies from without yourself. Then bringing them in to create a new energy from the combination of previous energies.

"Thank you. I want to learn to be friends with you," I wrote. "So how do I use the red petal formation?"

Just as you thought. Trace it with pencils. Hold the intention of what you desire: strength, centeredness, creativity, groundedness.

"Can you give me beautiful words for this formation?"

The Strength that You Truly Are—Stand in Your Strength and out of that strength create the greatest vision of yourself that you can be. Let the energy in you move toward that realization. That Strength in you. That Power. That Life. Beautiful Life.

The next day, after that message, I had a most illuminating dream. I was looking at a discarded full body mask that I had shed and left in the gutter in the streets of San Francisco. It was made of latex or rubber and had a doll's face. I took it to mean that I was shedding a layer of myself that was a mask. Then, I woke up singing "Too Legit To Quit, Too Legit to Quit," the MC Hammer rap song that the showy football player Deion Sanders would sing when he'd do something of note in a football game.

So, the meaning of this for me? As the words of the song say,

"I don't quit, no, I just press harder,
Than I ever did before going for,
The dreams I have in store in my mind."

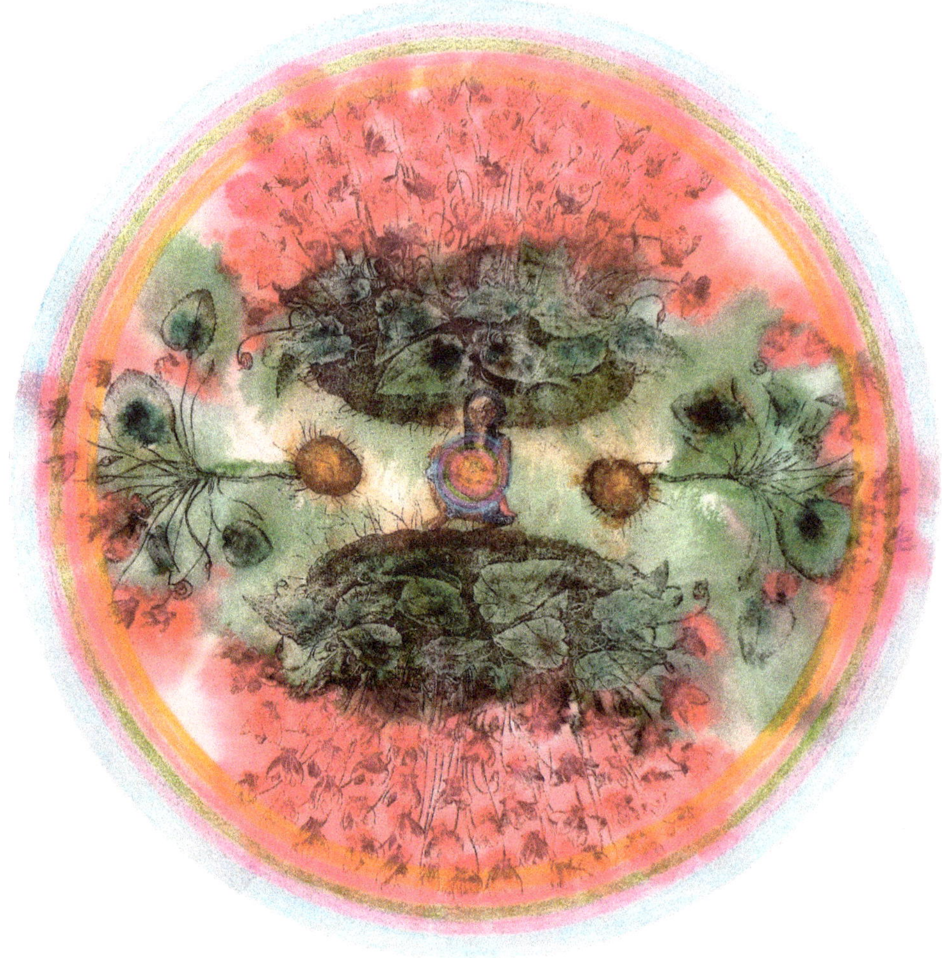

ABOUT THE PAINTING

"THE GODDESS WILL SEE YOU THROUGH"

Watercolor and colored pencil, 15" x 15" 2003

THE MESSAGE FROM THE FLOWERS SHOULD NOT BE IGNORED

"God, Guides, St. Germaine, Goddess: What am I to know today? How am I to follow my soul path?" I asked.

The phone rang and it was my mother. She told me that my aunt, who was an artist, had breast cancer. I started to cry.

"What's the matter? Why are you crying?" she said sounding annoyed with me.

"This is very difficult to hear and I feel bad for her," I said, reflecting on my own very hard journey, physically and emotionally through breast cancer. I was still so raw even after being finished with treatment for over a year. I reminded my mother once again that I had had a tough time.

"She'll be fine," she said about my aunt, with no emotion. Maybe my mother couldn't let herself feel any feelings about this news.

What the cancer treatment had done was open me up—I just couldn't hold any feelings down anymore like I'd learned to do my entire life. Old hurt, depression, anger, grief, loneliness and the feeling of being wrong flooded my consciousness. There was no place for any of these feelings while growing up, so I had stuffed them. I thought that I was a bad person for having feelings, and worked very hard at controlling them and tried not to have any. Well, the cancer treatments fixed that. Chemotherapy doesn't let you hold anything down! With all those old feelings coming forth, I felt bombarded. I went into panic attacks and at times didn't know if I could even survive, and at other times didn't want to. That is when I began intense psychotherapy. I really tried hard to understand that cancer had "saved my life" and that I had to learn to express myself and to have a voice.

I went to our art studio after that phone call and painted *The Goddess Will See You Through*. I wrote the intention for the painting on the back of the paper: "I intend to co-create with Spirit, a loving and healing mandala of the pink cyclamens I saw for the newborn." An Egyptian goddess had been coming into my mind's eye for some time, helping me, loving me and protecting me. In this painting the Goddess Isis is holding her baby at her breast, and I symbolically saw the baby as me. The concentric circles at the center of the Goddess are energizing both us and the cyclamens surrounding us, pink and electric, and are bringing energy to heal.

"You are my daughter," the Goddess told me. "I will save you."

Since starting to paint again, I processed old emotions with the inner images of a flower or flowers in a mandala. For at least two years, this process would almost always start with sobbing tears and very deep feelings. I used a lot of tissues during those times and joked that I ought to invest in Kleenex. But after the tears, I usually felt clear, cleaned out and empowered, and would begin on the mandala of flowers that I had seen from within.

The following day after the conversation with my mother and the completion of this painting, I had an appointment to see my homeopathic physician. I brought in two or three of my mandalas which "happened" to have cyclamens in them. He said that the cyclamen was used in homeopathy for those who felt they were always wrong and could never do anything right. He said the message from the flowers should not be ignored and gave me homeopathic cyclamen to take for awhile.

How perfect!

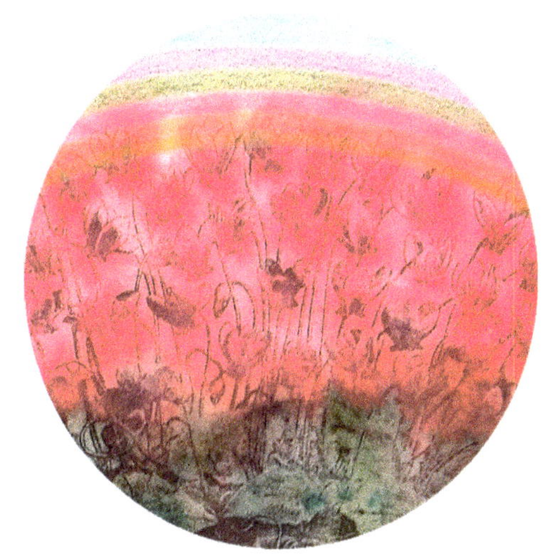

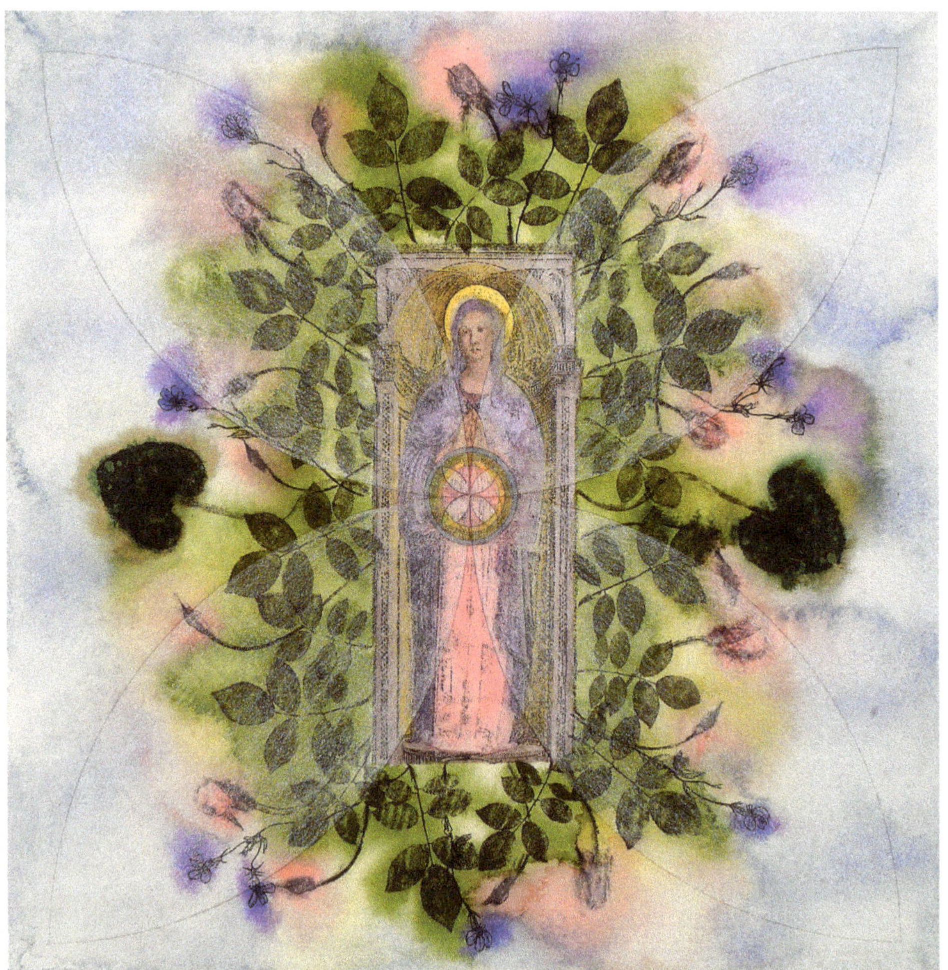

"Connecting With Mary: All Things Begin With This"

Ink transfer, watercolor, colored pencil, oil pastel, 15" x 15" 2003

Connections To Mary

Many years ago I brought a pastel drawing of my guardian angel to a frame shop to be framed. An intuitive had drawn her for me and she was definitely from another time. She was a beautiful and loving nun from a little town outside of Florence, Italy and she was drawn in very soft pastels. I truly felt like I knew her and had seen her "somewhere" before. The framer was fascinated by my story and the drawing. As we were finishing with the frame order, a couple came in with a huge print of Our Lady of Guadalupe, which they wanted framed. They obviously held her in reverence, and I told them I was also in the shop to have my guardian angel framed. The woman then told me the story of her connection to the Virgin. She said she herself had been still-born at birth, so her parents bundled her up, put her in a shoe box and put her on the shelf above the birth bed. They began to pray deeply to Our Lady of Guadalupe and soon the child "woke up." She had always felt Our Lady was her guardian angel. After the couple placed the frame order and left, the framer and I were completely amazed at what had just transpired. Two of his customers had exchanged stories of their guardian angels while time seemed to stand still.

Some years later, after my husband and I had moved back to the Santa Cruz area, I had the following dream. I was standing on a balcony at night and as I looked toward the ocean I saw something floating toward me on a cloud. As it got closer I saw that it was a white calla lily, and as it came overhead, it turned into the Virgin Mary. She was standing within an arch and was surrounded by little pink roses. She floated by and walked off into the clouds. I was very moved by this dream and wanted to paint her, but was unsure how to begin. I didn't paint people—and especially saints! The image of her was reminiscent of images I had seen in art history and so I finally did assemble her likeness by piecing together images I'd gathered in my art history books. That was how I created and painted my first Mary. This was during my dry spell from painting and I was frightened because some part of me felt that I was starting over. So being able to create this image of Mary was a big step and a fulfilling one. I entered the completed painting in an annual juried show, *Images of the Virgin*. The show was in a small woman's gallery, Galeria Tontanzin, in San Juan Bautista (one of the California Mission towns.) I felt honored to be in the show.

Before I began the painting, I asked Mary what she had to say:

In the painting, at Mary's center, I painted the four-petaled symbol, *Stand in Your Strength*, from Mandala One, page 88. It just seemed to belong there. The message I received, *"All Things Begin With This,"* seemed appropriate to be at Mary's center.

A friend sent me the book *A Handbook on Guadalupe*. In it the author investigated the imagery of the Virgin on Juan Diego's cloak. At Mary's womb was a four-petaled flower, the only one of that design on her tunic. The flower was identified as the Mexican four-petaled jasmine.

When I read this it confirmed to me that my vision of Mary with the flower at her center was the truth. The realization of it actually took my breath away!

Through the years I would paint an image or two of the Virgin, as I would get a vision, and enter one or more of them into the annual show at San Juan Bautista. And each year, since my granddaughter was three years old, we would bring her to the artists' reception. It became a tradition. She and I were connected in some way to this image—to Mary—to the Divine Mother. The images that I painted spoke to me very deeply and I felt like the messages I got really were directed to me. This is especially interesting because I was not raised Catholic and in our Protestant faith, Mary was just not revered as she was in Catholicism. At first that perplexed me, but then as I became more connected to her I simply enjoyed the comfort and that connection. I knew I was holding the link between my granddaughter and Mary, but was not sure exactly how. So, I just waited and watched.

MANDALA FOUR

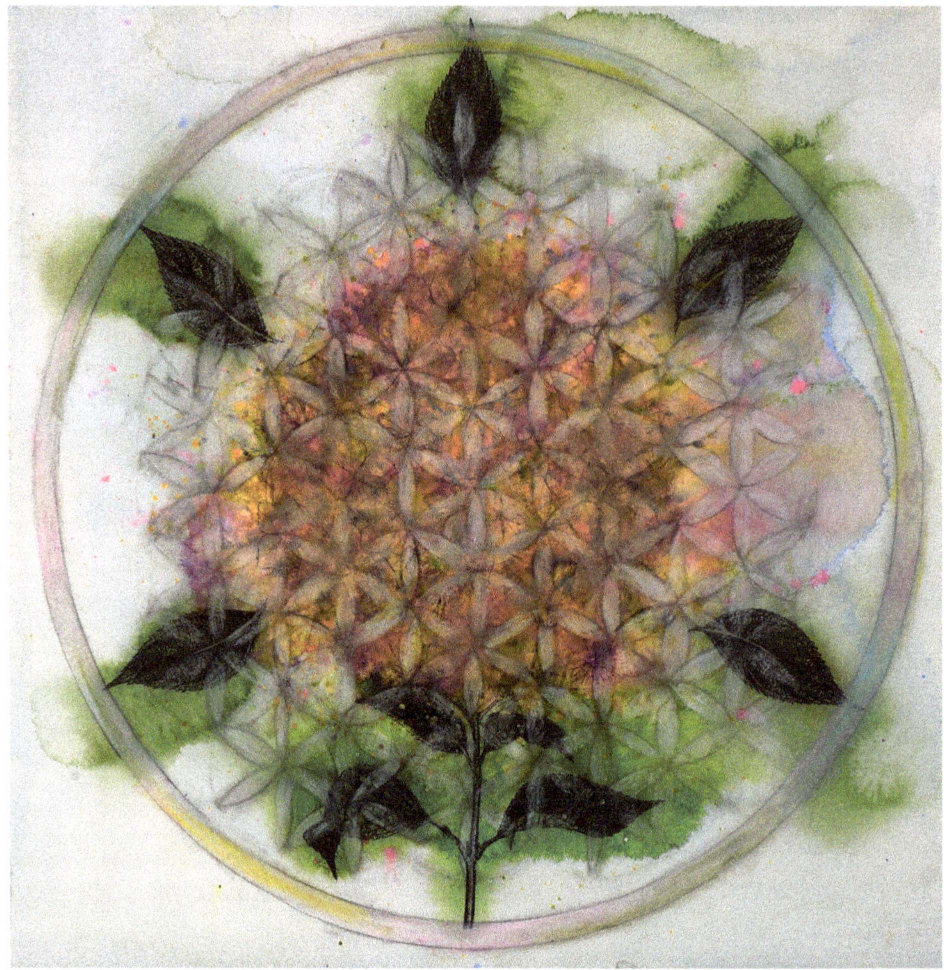

ABOUT THE PAINTING

"FULLNESS"

Ink transfer, watercolor, gouache, colored pencil, oil pastel, 15" x 15" 2004

WE ARE INTIMATELY CONNECTED TO THE SOURCE OF ALL LIFE

"It's OK to grow and bloom. It's OK to be who you are," I heard this within and wrote in my journal. It came from what felt like an inner spiritual guide.

This mandala, *Fullness*, is from a vision I had of a very large, white hydrangea blossom. As I saw it, it seemed that it represented one's fullest potential, to blossom fully and be oneself.

"What would that be like? What would I be like if I bloomed fully and purely?" I wondered.

"A vision of purity," I heard as I wrote.

"I imagine it would be a vision of such incredible beauty and light that it would be like the lyrics of a song 'Blinded by the Light,'" I wrote.

"Wouldn't that be something," I mused.

"How?" I asked.

I have heard for years from my guides, "Love yourself." Easier said than done, I think. But recently I have found that when I let that in, and really love myself, it is quite a calming, centering, wonderful experience.

One day I said to myself, "Oh, that's what it's supposed to feel like," when I experienced loving myself. And it did feel different than years of earlier attempts. It felt good, very good.

This mandala is a symbol of that state. Of being my fullest potential. In the painting I covered the blossom with drawings of a six-petaled pattern of sacred geometry. Sacred geometry is based on proportion; everything is in proportion, or a division of everything else. And all is a part of the divine whole.

The six-petaled pattern, which is easily done with a compass, is the beginning pattern of what is called the "Flower of Life." The Flower of Life pattern has been found all over the world in ancient artifacts and carvings. It is a pattern of nineteen, six-petaled patterns within a circle, and what it stands for and how it came to be in the places it has been found have long been a mystery. Drunvalo Melchizedek, in his books on the Flower of Life, says it shows that we are intimately connected to the source of all life.

I had been getting pieces of this pattern in visions for years and began including them in my mandalas. In this particular painting, I drew many six-petaled patterns connected, because one arises out of the other. It shows that these patterns are infinite—you could draw them and draw them and never come to the end because another pattern always arises.

In this mandala we see a representation of connection—connection to the source of all life, with infinite patterns. In this connection we are magnificent. Can we allow our awareness to blossom into its true magnificence, its truth and its beauty? Can we accept our connection to the Source?

Many of the mandalas I painted in this period were first created from pieces of images I put together as a collage before I painted. For this painting I photocopied leaves and flower blossoms from a hydrangea, sizing and moving them until I was satisfied with the arrangement. As always, I tried to stay true to the vision I had received. I transferred the black and white images onto the watercolor paper with a turpentine tool called a blender. I painted, colored and drew in layers on top of that design. This was a very comforting process for me and I think it was a metaphor for piecing myself back together.

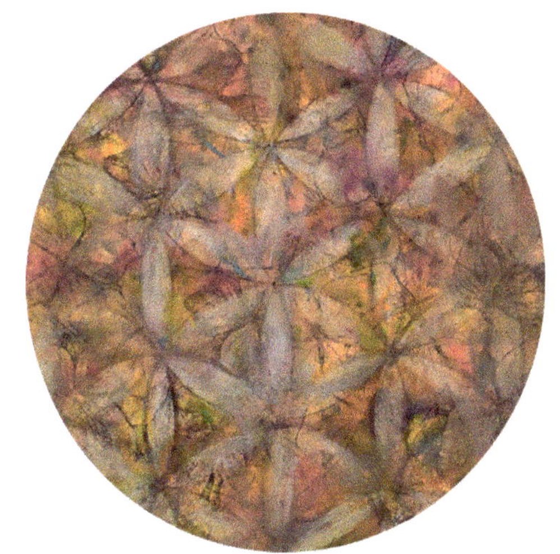

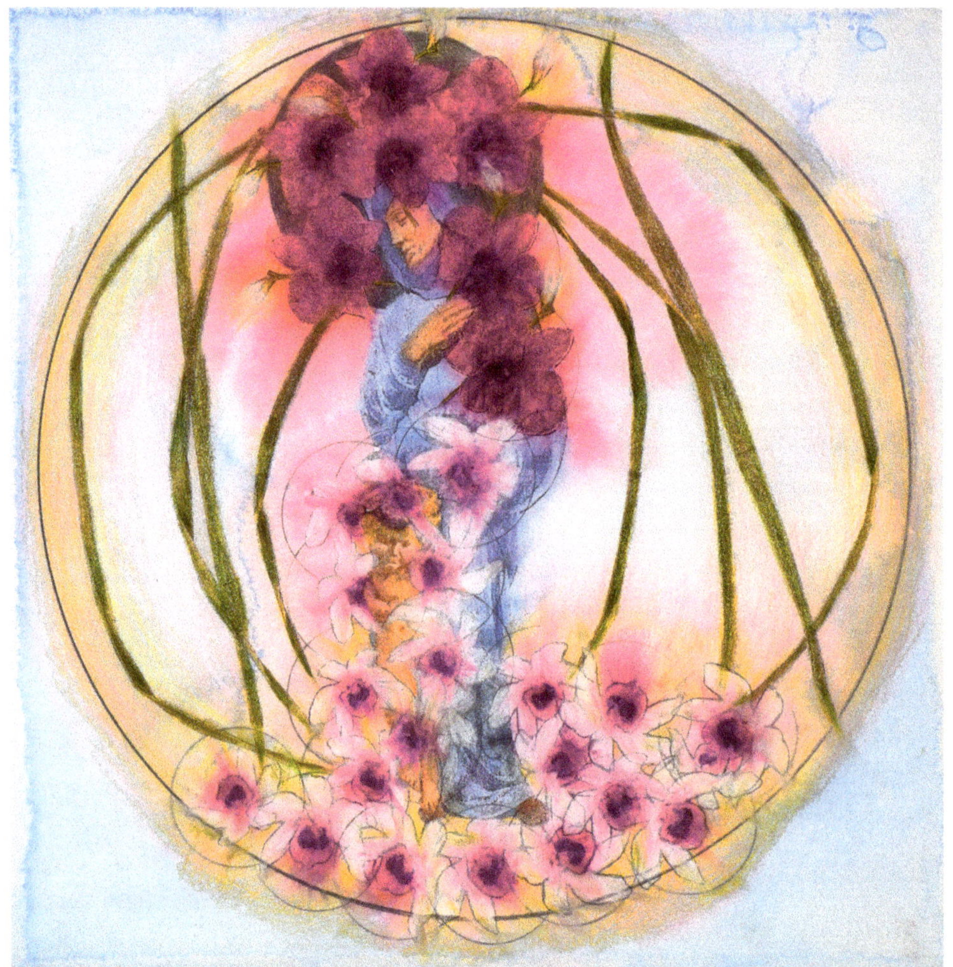

"THE TRANSFORMATION OF MARY"

Ink transfer, watercolor, colored pencil, oil pastel, 15" x 15" 2006

TRANSFORMED BY LOVE

Just before I painted this painting I had an interesting and revealing conversation with my homeopathic doctor.

"I didn't think I'd see you here for awhile, picking up the sword as you are, and not needing to be thrown a life raft or preserver," he said about seeing me standing stronger. He clearly liked seeing me like this. He asked me to repeat the mantra, "I am a powerful person."

"On your way to your true self you have to pass by and visit the wounded self. You are there," he said.

He continued, "You need to take time off to process and grieve. You are afraid to grieve—it wasn't OK to have grief."

"No sucking it up and getting resentful

anymore. Do not build any new resentments. Holding resentful energy leads to cancer. Work it through," he warned.

He said that my old habit of "numbing" myself by overeating chocolate was because, "Feelings would come up and you just couldn't feel them." I had to confess I would overeat chocolate when I lived alone, eating so much of it I would go into a fog and spend hours recovering.

When I painted this painting, *The Transformation of Mary*, I was feeling sad and emotional. My granddaughter had just returned home after spending a few days with us. These emotions almost always happened after she visited us, and I would cry and feel so empty and raw when she left.

"I don't like to feel this because it is so vulnerable," I wrote in my journal.

Then I saw an inner vision. It was a dendrobium orchid over the face of Mary. It was powerful and very beautiful. The orchid seemed to be me as a little girl, delicate and soft. It felt like it was a view of a part of me which had been hidden and was not at all like my usual self. I got the sense that this little girl felt vulnerable and afraid of wanting to be loved and cared for. It made me cry to feel the softness of the divine Mary taking care of and protecting me.

I asked, "Could someone like that really care for me?"

I heard, "Let the love in."

So my painting became a painting about transformation. Extreme transformation. Mary was transformed by the birth of Jesus, the incarnation of divine love, and I was being transformed by the love of Mary. It was a beautiful feeling and I felt so very honored.

This painting was shown one year in the *Images of the Virgin* show. And, of course, we took our granddaughter to the opening reception. I was being transformed as well by the love for my granddaughter.

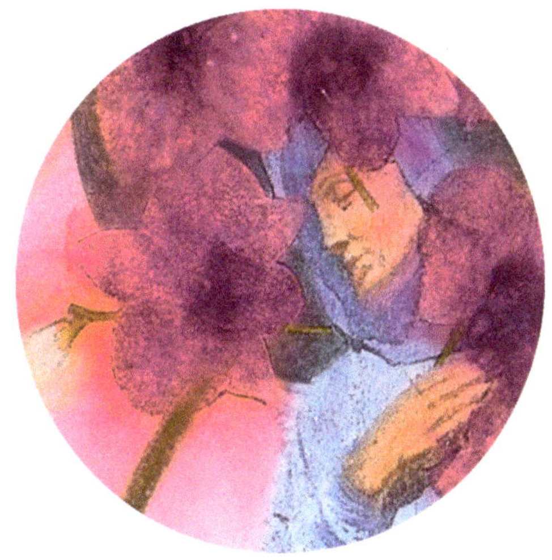

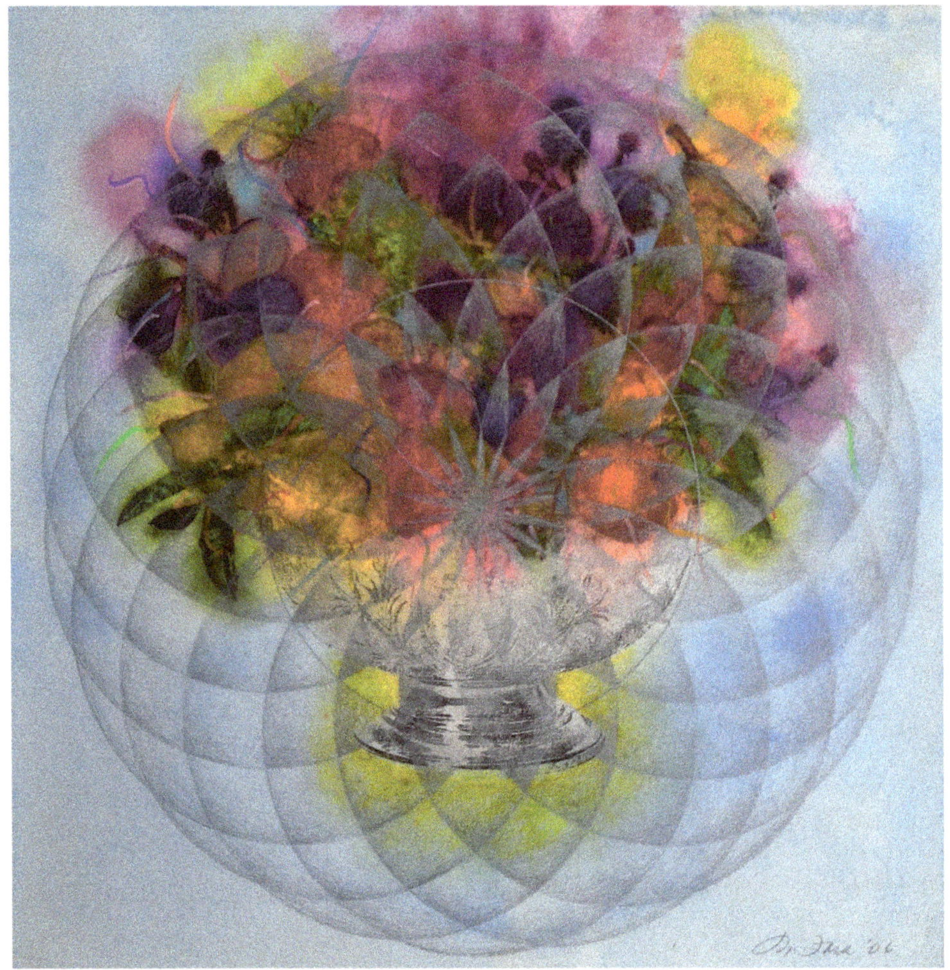

ABOUT THE PAINTING

"EXPLODING BERRIES: FINDING MY WAY TO THE CONNECTION OF THE UNIVERSE"

Ink transfer, watercolor, gouache, colored pencil, oil pastel, silver felt pen, 15" x 15" 2006

THE CHALICE OF THE HEART

"The berries burst. The bubbles burst. The boundaries burst. Finding my way to the connection of the universe." That is what I wrote on the back of this painting before I started it. The mandala is a chalice full of fruit—lemons, grapes, peaches, pears, strawberries, blackberries, raspberries. They seemed to want to explode—to burst beyond their boundaries. It is a joyous explosion, about energy that cannot be contained any longer. And, in its breaking of boundaries, it joins other energies in the universe and connects on a higher level with the cosmos.

The chalice is silver and I remember reading a best-selling novel, *The Silver Chalice*, when I was in junior high school and loved it. It was the story of an artist, a silversmith, who worked and worked to create a chalice for the Holy Grail. I loved the story of creating this sacred vessel and somehow participating in the spiritual mystery of it.

Prior to painting this mandala I had been feeling "trapped." I wanted to be free of my tendency to try and fix others. That's what I grew up doing, trying to fix my sick younger brother or be perfect for my mother. How is a child going to do either of these? I thought it would bring me love.

I wrote in my journal, "Goddess—what do I do? I need help."

So here is an explosion of that pattern of mine. "Breaking Free" would have also been a good title, breaking the boundaries in order to connect with the higher self.

As usual, the painting came from an inner vision. I must say it was rather wild seeing this explosion in my inner eye, berry juice spraying and all. Sometimes when something unusual like this happens, I'll want to push it aside and ignore it. This one wouldn't go away.

"What is this? I thought. "What the heck. Well, I'll have to think about the meaning of this later!"

I can't think about the meaning of the mandalas as I paint them, I'm just busy staying true to the vision. Then later I'll piece it all together. It's kind of like unraveling the meaning of a dream. It's not straight forward, it's definitely a process and I'm always fascinated with the journey. The unraveling speaks in symbols and always has an emotion or emotions attached to it. That is where I usually find the key to the meaning: *It's in the emotions in the heart, in the center of the heart, in the chalice of the heart where a kind of communion happens. It's where you can have an intimate spiritual relationship with yourself and God, Goddess, All That Is. It's where the transformation happens when you hold the light that is already inside of you. For me it's where the message comes, where the emotions heal, where meaning is unveiled. It's where peace is found and your beautiful self revealed.*

I could not see my beautiful self while I was living in my old patterns and my old self, and that did not serve me.

So the bubble burst!

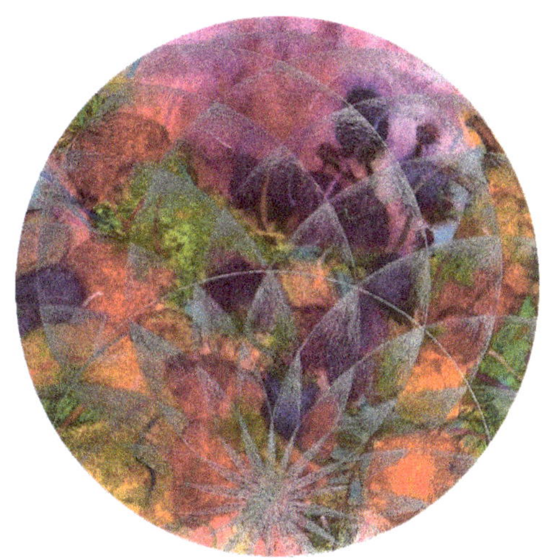

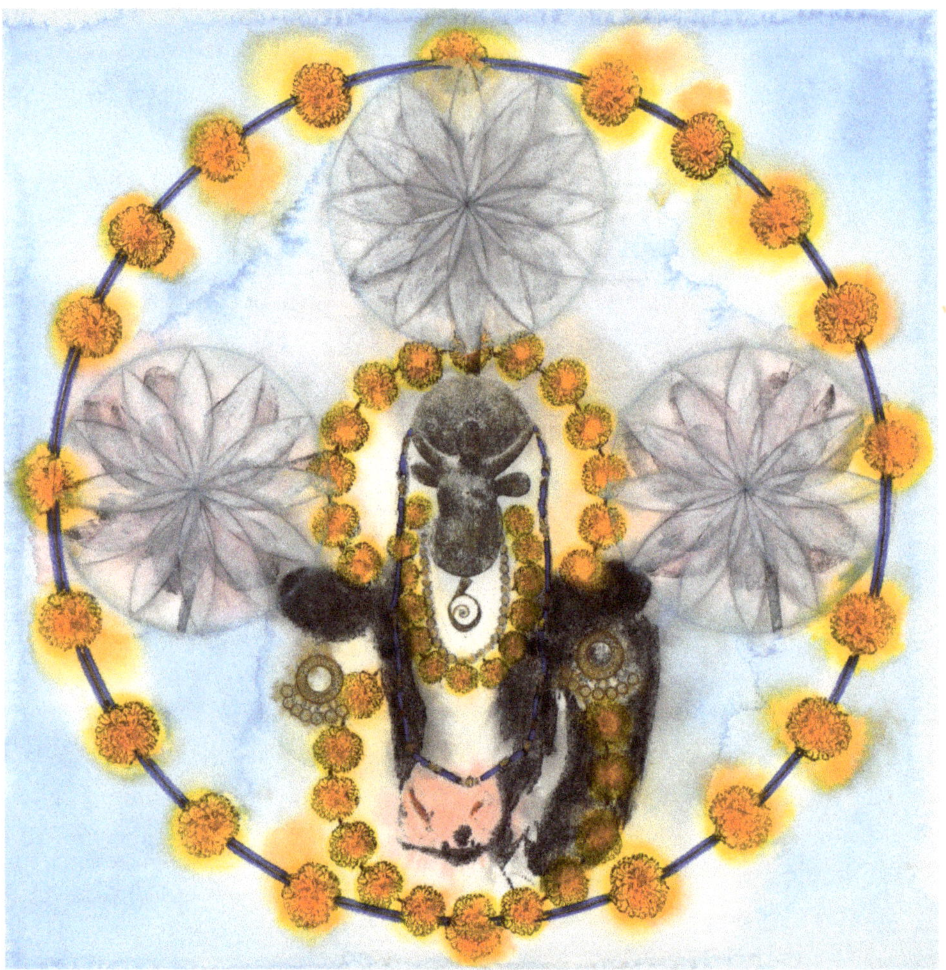

About the Painting

"Holy Cow! I'm Being Re-Mothered"

Ink transfer, watercolor, colored pencil, oil pastel, 15" x 15" 2006

Awakening From A Long Sleep

This painting is of a sweet cow which I loved adorning with gold earrings, a garland of marigolds and a crown of jewels. On her head is the Egyptian goddess Hathor, symbolic of the life-giving Great Mother with her sacred cow imagery. Above her are lotuses, and all of it is surrounded by a wreath of marigolds. The dictionary says that the origin of the word marigold "is probably Virgin Mary + gold."

When I was a child my grandparents had a dairy ranch. Cows have always been symbolic to me of the wonderful, unconditional love I received from my grandparents. They left me way too soon, both dying of brain cancer the same year, when I was six. I don't believe I really ever got over the grief of their loss. Everyone—my teacher, my parents, and the school kids were too busy with other more important matters to notice how devastated I was by the loss of my grandparents' security, love and support. I cried a lot and the kids called me "Cry Baby." I hated that and determined then that I would toughen up! Many years later I wrote in my journal about my grandmother's death: "I became so angry at myself for not being able to control my emotions."

As a little girl I felt embarrassed that I wanted help and comfort and worked very hard at not wanting it. I tried to be self-sufficient, having learned it was a sign of weakness to ask for help. Everyone around me was preoccupied. It was such an inner conflict for me because I wanted love, but hated myself for wanting it. I worked so hard at denying my feelings and pushing away any love that would come my way, feeling I didn't deserve it. The loneliness was just devastating.

My twenties were spent reading lots of self-help books, always trying to figure out what was the matter with me for being unloveable. When did the light bulb go on to make me at least begin to realize that I was OK and that those thoughts about myself were not true?

It happened in a meditation class with my first attempt to meditate. Wow, what an experience! I saw the light inside of me and it was just incredible. That was the beginning of my spiritual search. I wanted to continue seeing that light and feeling and knowing that all was right with me and the world.

"However perfect motherly love will be, it is not self-love, and for many years you will sigh over the loss of perfect love, only to realize that you are nostalgic for your own self before anyone else arrived on the scene." (Deepak Chopra, *The Way of the Wizard*, 1995, pg.152.)

With this painting I believe I was acknowledging a rebirth of myself—with whimsy, playfulness and light-heartedness. It was a spiritual rebirth through the Divine Mother, as symbolized by the cow. It took me a long time to accept mothering and love—I was afraid the love would die and leave me.

"There are those of you...whose lives are controlled by the fear of abandonment. The windows of opportunity come your way to correct this, yet you do not go through them....When these situations occur, we invite you to walk straight into them! The tool you now carry is the love of God in the New Energy. This love is all around you. Your guides and angels stand beside you and hold your hands whether you are in the most barren part of Earth or the most populous. Feel this anointed love surround you. Claim it! Cross this painful bridge, feel the love pour into you, and know that abandonment is not in your program any longer. Feel the magnetic code dissipate as you free yourself from this phantom, and know that you are cared for by an energy that will never, ever abandon you. Your efforts will be rewarded with success, for this is the lesson, and the passing of it will raise your vibration and that of the entire planet!" (Lee Carroll, *The Parables of Kryon*, 1996, pg.115.)

One day when I was a child visiting my grandparents, I came across a calf laying motionless on the grass and thought it was dead. Frantically, I ran to my grandmother only to be comforted and reassured by her that the calf was just asleep.

No, my divine self had not been dead either. It had been awakening from a long sleep. Holy cow, I claim it!

MANDALA EIGHT

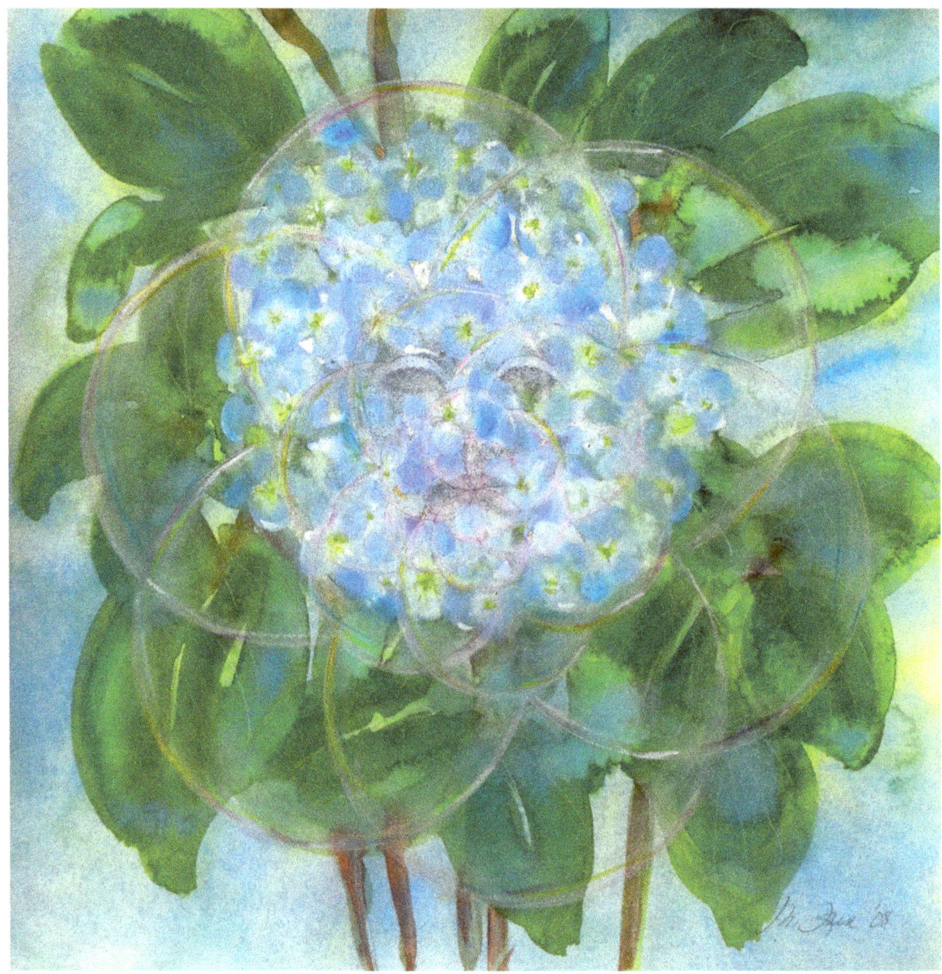

"Her Face Is In Every Flower"

Ink transfer, watercolor, gouache, colored pencil, oil pastel, 15" x 15" 2008

The Face In The Flower

I had been seeking an answer to this question, "Who is the Mother of God?"

I saw a woman's face coming through a blue hydrangea blossom and heard, "Her face is in every flower."

The face seemed ancient and Egyptian. And of course I asked myself, "How do I paint that?"

I searched for some time to find the essence of the "right" face which I had seen. I settled on a beautiful Egyptian queen. As I proceeded with the work, I drew the hydrangea leaves free hand and painted them in a loose and spontaneous way. Then I created the hydrangea itself by piecing together petals to create the full blossom. I wanted the sacred geometry pattern over the whole piece to look like a flower that multiplied out, like pebbles in a pond, rippling from the center.

Why did I ask that question, "Who is the Mother of God," in the first place? The answer I got to my question was unexpected, and amazing to me.

I had been seeing so many different visions of Mary and I couldn't help but wonder, "Why and why me?" I was certainly not a follower of any traditional religion. Clearly there was a lot about a "mother" that was surfacing in my life which came with a particular period of loneliness. Because of that I had been wondering if a person could ever heal the loneliness. I was definitely walking straight through these feelings as the previous Kryon writing suggested to do. The answers to my questions were coming in the form of God, Mother and flowers. It got my attention I suppose. I was surrounded—flowers were everywhere in my life. How could I miss the answer?

"Beauty is life when life unveils her holy face.
But you are life and You are the veil.
Beauty is eternity gazing at itself in the mirror.
But You are eternity and you are the mirror."
(Kahil Gibran, *The Prophet,* 1968, pg. 76)

"And just whose face is it in the flower?" I was asked.

"Yours!" I heard.

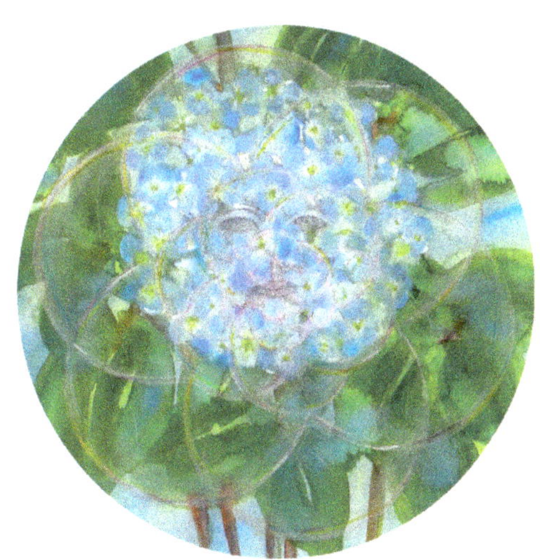

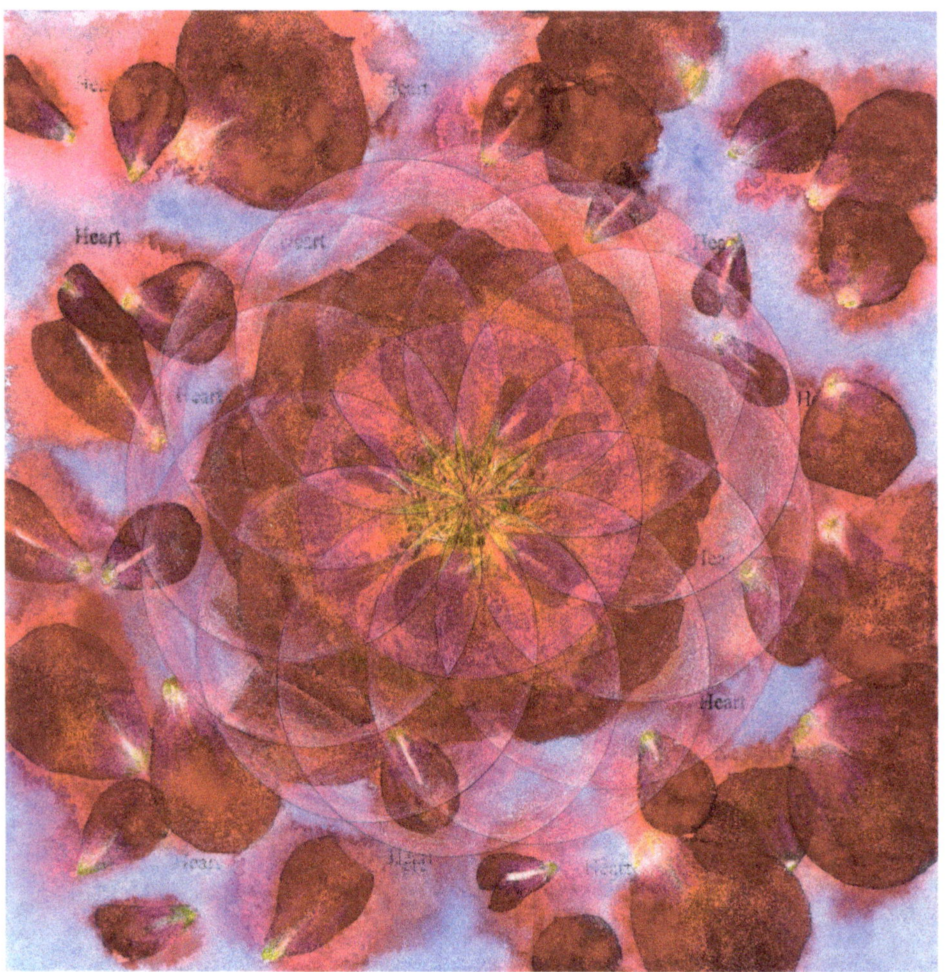

ABOUT THE PAINTING

"THE ROSE IN MY HEART II"

Ink transfer, watercolor, gouache, colored pencil, oil pastel, 7.5" x 7.5" 2008

HERE'S THE ROSE AGAIN

It was getting to be that time of year again when we would go to the annual artist's reception and opening for the *Images of the Virgin* show at Galleria Tonantzin. My work was being accepted each year and we continued to bring my granddaughter to the shows which were birthday celebrations honoring the Virgin of Guadalupe. This year we decided to take in the play, *Virgin of Tepeyac*, put on by El Teatro Campesino at the San Juan Bautista Mission Church. We drove to San Juan Bautista ahead of time to buy tickets for the play and when I walked into the ticket office I was overwhelmed and choked up with emotions. The poster for the play had rose petals on it, referring to the roses on the cloak of Juan Diego. It just struck me—the rose again! Oh my God! It's always connected to my granddaughter.

I thought, "Those rose petals are activating the rose in my heart, which I had originally seen following my granddaughter's birth. How is this all connected—Mary, my granddaughter, and me?"

Then I felt my chest fill up with roses. It was just incredible. I had the thought that the Mother was leaving an impression on my heart as she had done so long ago in Juan Diego's beautiful vision of our Lady of Guadalupe. As I grasped for meaning, I wondered if that could be possible.

The truth is that something happens at this time every year to me and my granddaughter at Our Lady of Guadalupe's birthday (December 12th.) I have seen that my heart opens a little wider each time and it always feels so very profound!

I painted this painting with the word "heart" repeated in the background several times. I did it during the holiday season, just before Our Lady's birthday. It had to wait a year before I submitted it for acceptance in the annual *Images of the Virgin* show. And, it was accepted and exhibited. The painting really belongs to my granddaughter and I will give it to her when I can fully explain the meaning it has for both of us. But I don't think I fully know what that is yet.

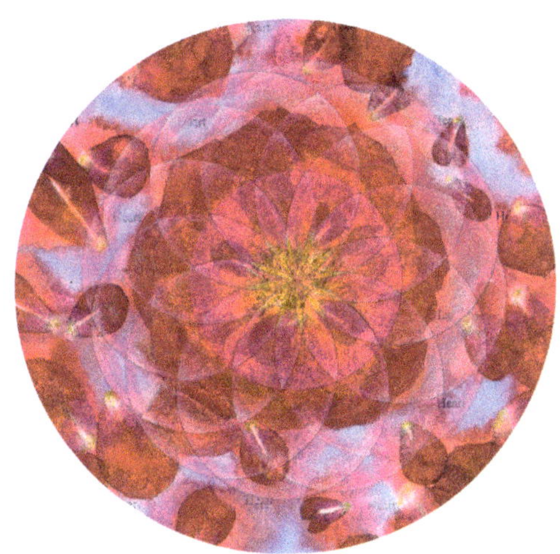

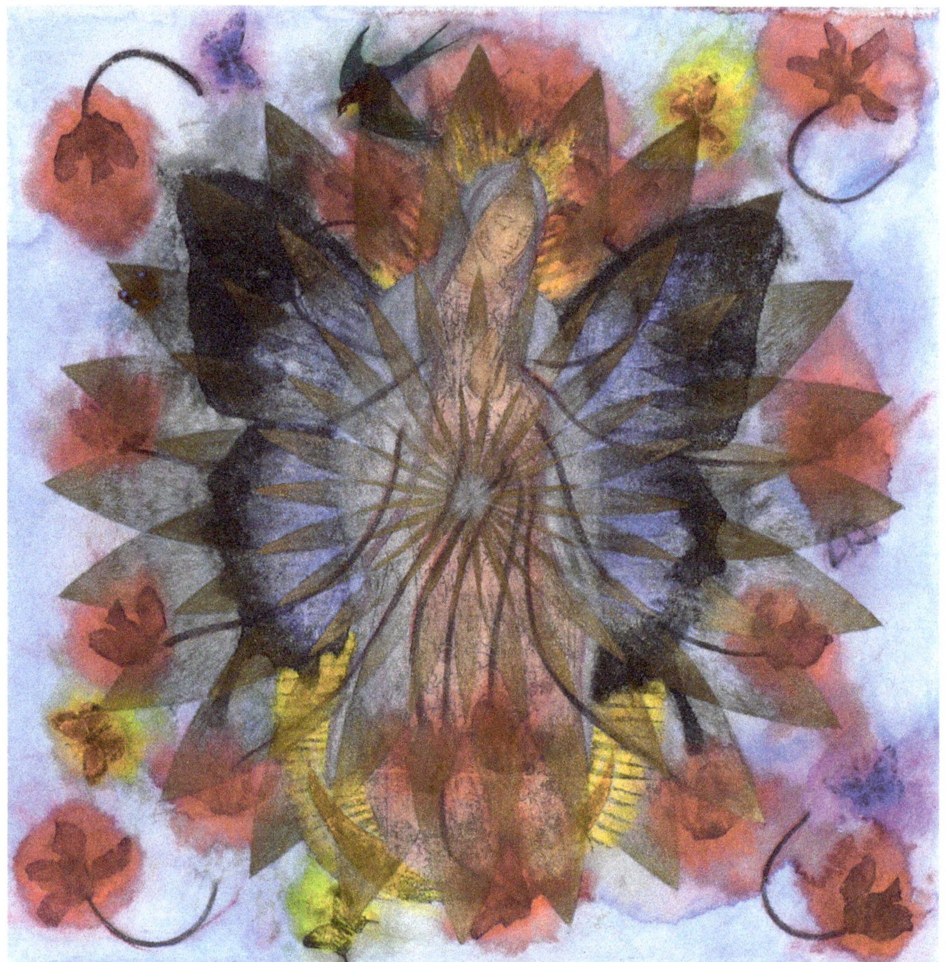

ABOUT THE PAINTING

"METAMORPHOSIS"

Ink transfer, watercolor, gouache, colored pencil, 15" x 15" 2010

LOVE IS ALL AROUND

Before going into my cancer treatments, and after my surgeries, I consulted a medical intuitive to see what she saw as my prognosis.

"You're going to be fine," she said, immediately preferring to talk about the help I was being given from my unseen spiritual guides, one of which was Mary.

This surprised me because, at the time, I couldn't believe Mary even knew who I was. The intuitive told me to take Mary with me to my treatments and she would help me.

Mary said to me, "I love you. When will you love you?"

She was right. She did know who I was!

Before I received the vision in this painting, I was being assailed with old self-critical thoughts again. It felt like they were taking me down and I was getting depressed.

One night, during the time that I lay awake before sleeping, the thought suddenly came to me: "I can do this. Mary will help. My mother inside will help me." Such peace came over me and I fell asleep.

The next day I questioned, "Goddess, Mary, can you help me?"

They answered, "Let us help you. Let go. Stop arguing (that it will never work out.) We are here. We will help. You can relax."

This brought me to tears and I persisted in wondering, "Could this really happen?"

I then heard the verse of an old rock n' roll song by The Troggs:

"I feel it in my fingers, I feel it in my toes

Love is all around, and so the feeling grows."

Wow! What was going on?

"There is a little girl inside who needs to feel her feelings and that is hard," I wrote in my journal.

Following that introductory music, I saw a vision of Mary, as Our Lady of Guadalupe, covered with flowing red cyclamen blossoms. The flowers felt like they were bursting forth from a seed, a seed cracking open its protective shell and pouring forth life energy which needed to expand. I saw big silvery-blue butterfly wings come out of Our Lady. It seemed that it was a birth, a metamorphosis, the painful opening out of a cocoon. I sobbed hard for the vulnerable little girl inside who was letting go of the grief which had been held for so long and could no longer be contained. I knew I needed to "feel it to heal it," as one of my earlier mandala paintings had once suggested. Then I saw rays of light exploding from Mary's center. The greatest life force was bursting from her, and it was shining on me and out to the world. It was so beautiful and powerful that I cried. I knew that all would be well and that she would help me heal. And, I did discover with great joy, "Love is all around, and so the feeling grows."

I exhibited the painting in the annual *Images of the Virgin* show. After the show, a woman who had seen it called me.

"Is it still for sale?" she inquired.

"Yes it is," I said, having just asked myself where I was going to put it.

"We want it," she said, acting as a spokesperson for a peace garden in Hawaii.

It was purchased and now hangs in Paleaku Gardens Peace Sanctuary on the big island of Hawaii. The gardens sold giclée prints of this painting as a fundraiser for the Sanctuary. A woman from the gardens told me she felt *Metamorphosis* represented the coming forth of more feminine energy on the planet, and that they had been searching for such a representation of Mary.

The whole experience was a most powerful one for me.

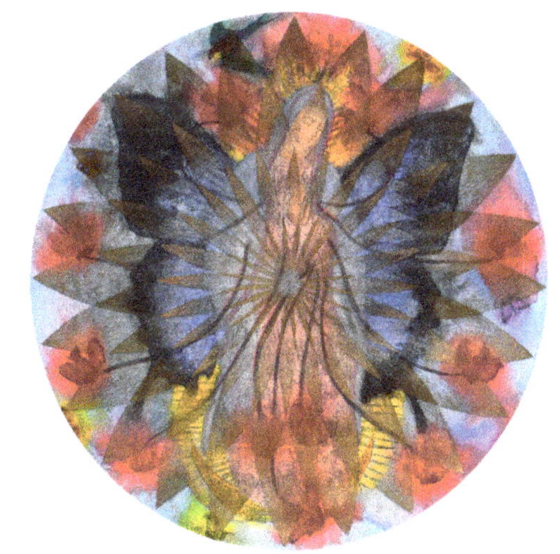

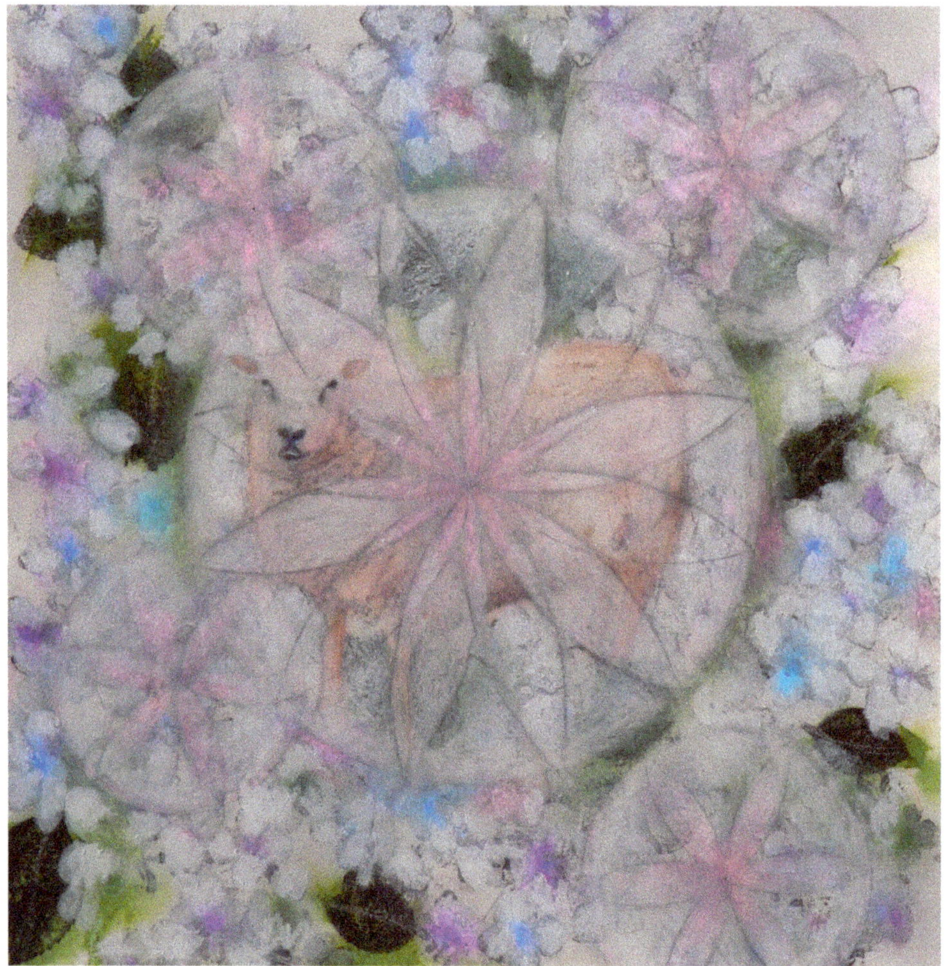

ABOUT THE PAINTING

"EWE WITH A MESSAGE"

Ink transfer, watercolor, gouache, colored pencil, oil pastel, 8.5" x 8.5" 2011

WITH A LITTLE HELP FROM MY FRIENDS

The ewe came to me in the early hours of one New Year's morning. I like to ask for a message or an image for the New Year as I go to sleep on New Year's Eve. But, it wasn't clear right off what the meaning of it was for me.

Truthfully, I'd had something on my mind—a mandala I wanted to paint and I wasn't sure of the imagery for it. The image of the ewe somehow seemed to fit. When I'd become aware of the events around the shooting of U.S. Representative Gabby Giffords and the others in Arizona, I wanted to do something. As I listened to one of her doctors on TV talk about how she was already doing better than expected, I was touched by a candid comment one of them made. He said something to the effect that he didn't know if he believed in such things, but that having good caring friends, like she had, was having a positive effect on her recovery and she was doing better than expected.

"Of course it does," I thought, remembering the time I was helped and healed of a serious health complication by a group of caring friends.

"OK," I thought. "I'm going to do a mandala for her and tell her my experience—how wonderful and miraculous the possibility of healing can be from those who love you."

It had been about eight years since my cancer experience. But, completely by chance, a mysterious spot was found in my lung when I'd gone in for some stomach problems and had a CT scan. It put everyone on alert. More tests were scheduled, and more doctors to see. My friend Maggie "happened" to stop by to see me at work, and when she heard the news about the spot, she got on the phone to an old friend who was a medical intuitive on a radio show. The woman told her that my "spot" was extremely dangerous and that I needed to get it out of there ASAP! She said it was where I had stuffed my negative emotions throughout my life.

"So," she emphasized, "no more stuffing."

I knew I needed to step up my releasing of old emotions. I stopped being so cavalier about the whole thing and suggested to Maggie that maybe I could ask a group of my mandala students for help. For me that was difficult. I was a helper, but I never asked others for it—and frankly wondered if it would actually help me anyway. Just the week before a group of women had come to my studio for a drop-in mandala class and our theme that day was light. Maggie emailed the group we called the Circle of Light, and asked the seven women to send me light.

"Michele has always been so generous about her light, but now she's the one who needs it," she wrote.

Everyone responded. It was about a two month process before I had a lung biopsy, with trips to different doctors and clinics. I was actually uncomfortable in the hot seat with the attention on me. In a way, I felt guilty for taking people's time, and I wanted it to be over quickly. But during that time I consciously worked on not stuffing my emotions which meant that I was feeling lots of emotions. Everyone was so wonderful—friends, family and doctors. Finally I had the biopsy, which went smoothly, and the lab report was negative—they didn't know what it was, but it wasn't cancer! So I called Maggie's intuitive friend and told her the good news.

"That's great," she said, "Because you knew it was malignant, didn't you?"

"No!" I said, very shocked by this news. "Maggie didn't tell me that! Well, actually I'm glad she didn't—I probably would have focused on that and the fear, and not on the work I needed to do."

The woman continued. "When something in the body is going through a spiritual change, it does not register or show up in the traditional way. But when a report says it is of 'unknown origin,' that is the clue that it is changing, and that is excellent news!"

I was ecstatic—and also still in shock over the seriousness of the situation. I went for a CT scan six months later because the doctors wanted to monitor the spot. But it was gone—disappeared! Needless to say, I was euphoric.

So when I had seen the doctor refer to Gaby's "friends" in the TV news conference, I had a deep emotional response to it.

I thought, "It's true, it does work. Her friends are helping her and it's making a difference. The doctors are noticing. It happened to me and I was healed. I was helped—I had never asked for help from my friends before. I asked and they helped me. It worked."

It cinched my belief in miracles and miracle healings, what light and love can do and how we can all help each other.

I recently had the occasion to pass this on to another friend. His wife had commissioned me to do a mandala painting for his new office. But in the meantime he got severely ill and was going in for a life-threatening surgery. Before the surgery he spoke to me about how he'd watched me go through my illness and admired how I'd weathered it and grew from the experience. I told him that I had a lot of help, especially during the lung challenge. I told him that he had an opportunity for great healing because of all the many, many friends he'd made around the world, being a visionary and pioneer in his field. And then I told him about Gabby Giffords and how her friends and family (and of course, her many doctors) helped her through her recovery. He got emotional about that. I would imagine if he is anything like me, it was hard to ask for help when you have been the helper of so many—and he certainly had been.

He did have his surgery, and it was very difficult, and at times his situation was extremely grave. But, he came through it and eventually he contacted me so that he could pick up his mandala. He was returning to work and wanted it for his office.

"The miracle continues," he said.

So, like a pebble in the pond, the rippled healing effect keeps touching others' lives. I will never let it stop if it's up to me. Now when I hear of a friend who is going through a challenge, if nothing else, I will send them light. And if I am able and it is appropriate, I will do a little 3" or 4" mandala for them with the intention of light, love and healing for them. I call them "Circles of Love." That's something I can do and I think that the people I give them to feel good about it, and I know that I sure do.

I have kept Gabby's mandala for quite a long time, not mailing it to her, and wondering why. I realized that I wanted to make a print of it for each of the women who helped me. I want them to really know how much they helped me, how deeply grateful I am to all of them, and that I am grateful to be able to pass it on!"

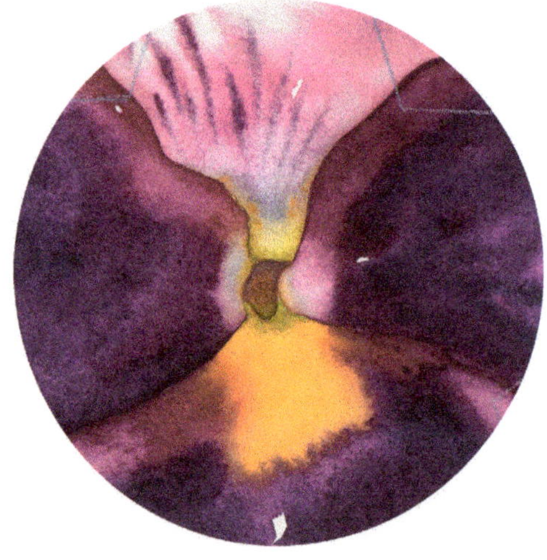

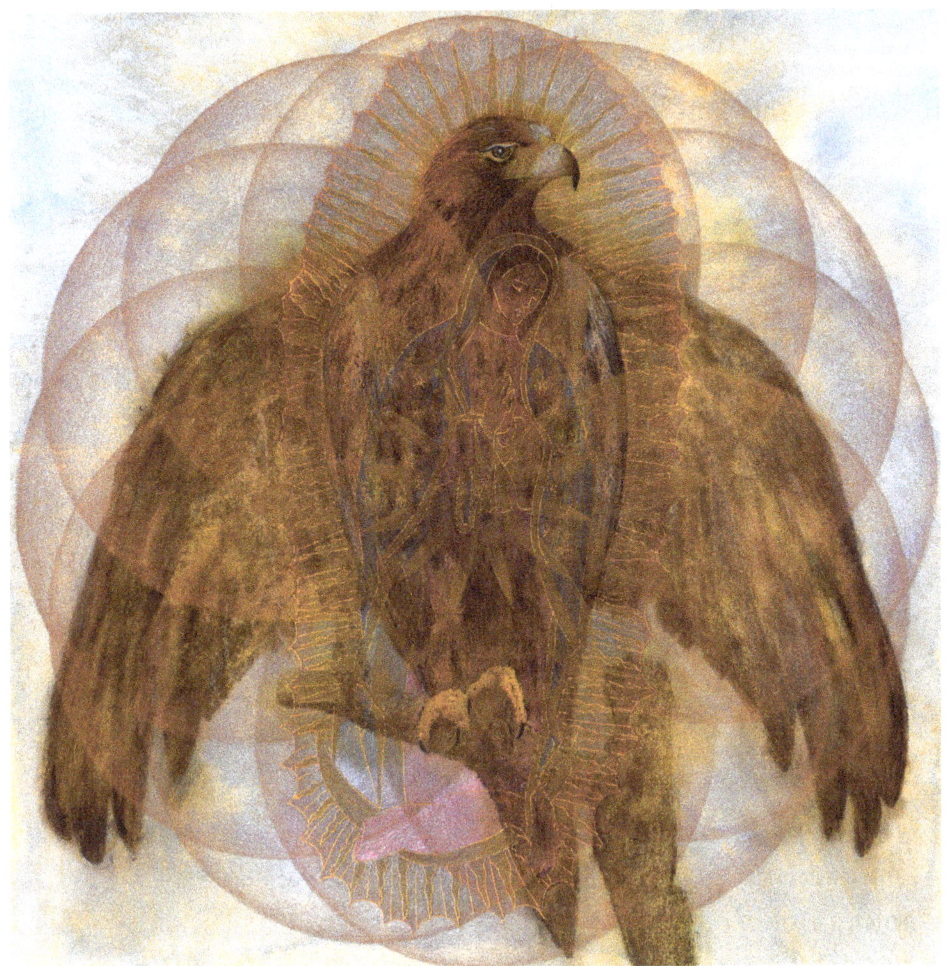

ABOUT THE PAINTING

"THE VISION OF THE EAGLE WHO SINGS"

Ink transfer, watercolor, colored pencil, gold foil, 15" x 15" 2011

THE MESSENGER OF LOVE

This image of the eagle with the Virgin of Guadalupe on its chest actually came to me before I received the image for the painting *Metamorphosis*. It was such a powerful image but I didn't understand why it had come to me. It seemed to be an image that was bigger than life, and I was reluctant to even attempt to paint it.

In fact, I wasn't going to attempt it at all, and then it just happened.

I looked for an image of the "right" eagle that I could use as I collaged the painting together before I started to paint. It was clearly a golden eagle—big, majestic and powerful. I couldn't find an eagle which would work, so I pieced one together from different sources. It seemed to have strong male energy and had wings that were starting to open, but were not in a full wingspan. The Virgin seemed to fit perfectly on the eagle's chest between the wings, nestled and protected there. I actually was enjoying the challenge of creating this piece and I went slowly and deliberately—which was not always my way of working.

The actual watercolor painting of it, getting the color and the feel of the feathers, was dicey. Then came the problem of how to show the Virgin coming through as a visionary impression on the eagle's chest. It was my husband who suggested I use gold foil and outline the halo. I tried that and applied the foil with a hot stylus, something I'd never done before—and it worked. The final addition to the painting was the circular sacred geometry mandala around the eagle and the Virgin. That was drawn using a compass and a copper colored pencil.

When the painting was finished it surprised me, and I thought, "I did it! But, Oh My God, what does it mean?" I was not aware of a connection between the Virgin and an eagle, so I Googled it. No surprise. The meaning of the man's name who received the vision of Our Lady on his shawl so many hundreds of years ago, Juan Diego, is "the eagle who sings." I liked how the clues were being beautifully pieced together for me like I pieced together the eagle.

I was scheduled for a weekend art show in the garden where I work part time, so I framed the painting and displayed it for the first time. Some customers told me it was too hard to look at, and others said they liked it. One woman, not familiar with a mandala, asked me if a mandala was a maze. I told her a mandala was more like a labyrinth, and suggested she try walking one where she could immerse herself physically in it. (Coincidently, I had just heard of a labyrinth in the town where she was from and where I had been three days earlier giving an art talk.)

The woman went on to say that her brother had liked eagles, past tense. She quietly and painfully said he had just died. She bought a print of the painting, all the cards I had, and ordered more. She said she wanted to give one to each of her nieces and nephews. She thanked me profusely and said she had not wanted to come that day, but a friend suggested she get out and she was extremely glad she had. She said she somehow felt guided by and connected to her brother when she saw my painting.

I am so glad that the painting spoke to her and it certainly gave the mandala even more meaning to me as well. This experience seemed to be a lot about following and trusting our guidance. In this case, this woman and I were brought together in time, and in a way that was beyond each of our comprehension. As I contemplated the meaning of what had happened, the word "messenger" came to me. It was so quick and brief that I almost ignored it. Then I remembered a message I received by email that morning from my friend Lee Carroll who writes the Kryon books.

"Kryon teaches us that intuitive energy is the way spirit talks to us, but we often wait and wait even after it's over...thinking it was only our own thoughts, and we discount it....It's a great time... to begin to listen to those beautiful instructions that God gives us for our lives. Don't discount "first intuition," for it may be the entire fireworks show in a flash...and be the guidance you have been waiting for." (Lee Carroll, *Upclose Family Bulletin*, July 2012 Update.)

This painting seems to be about a long line of messages. I originally got a message by way of a vision. It connected to a past event in which a simple young man, Juan Diego, received a message from Our Lady and he was asked to pass it on to the powers that be and then on to the people. Her message was that a church was to be built on the spot where she had appeared and would be for everyone, so that everyone could have access to her. I think the message lives on. She is here for everyone. My experience was that I felt such wonderful and unconditional love and complete protection and acceptance. I felt her love for me deeply. She is a messenger of love.

The woman whose brother liked eagles mentioned that her nephew was going to get an eagle tattoo in honor of his dad. I asked her if it might be possible to get a photograph of it, and she sent it to me.

After that, I decided I wanted to go and walk the labyrinth myself.

That story is in Mandala Fourteen, page 116.

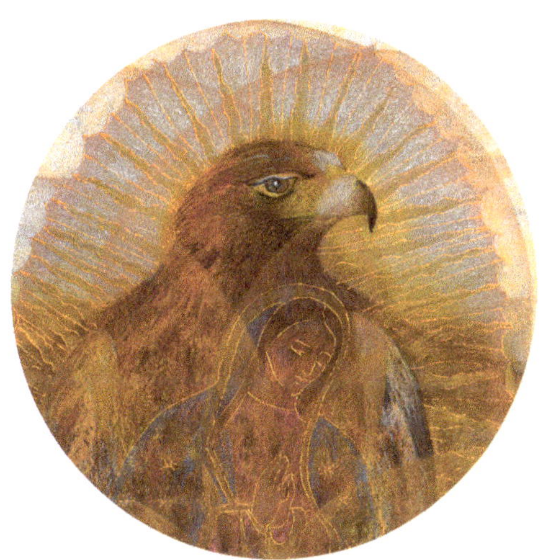

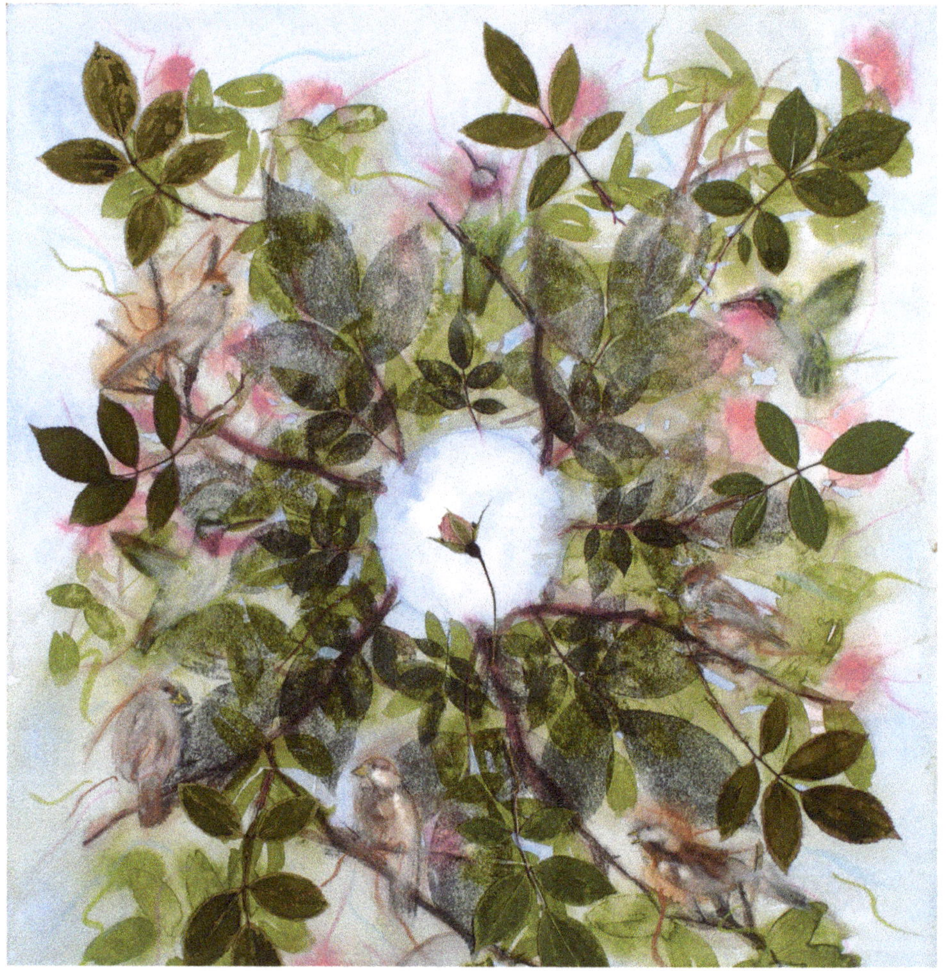

ABOUT THE PAINTING

"The Birds Came"

Ink transfer, watercolor, gouache, colored pencil, oil pastel, dried rose and leaves, 15" x 15" 2011

The Truth Will Set You Free

The day the birds came and sang their hearts out was a significant one for me. I had written in my journal, "I woke up sad and the birds came. I saw little birds in my Cecile Brunner rose trees. I saw the rose leaves and the budding pink roses and the birds came in—there were lots of sparrows and even a hummingbird."

I really hate waking up sad. It is really hard to feel grief and I don't like it at all. I am told it is the hardest emotion to feel. Because it is so hard, it is easier to feel other emotions instead. For me that was anger. I was full of grief, but it looked like anger. I found I'd do just about anything not to feel my grief. It's kind of like throwing up. I just don't want to let it go, but after I do, I feel so much better.

As a little girl I felt rejected and left out when my brother was born. He was the first and only son, and I felt he was favored. He may not have been, but I felt like he was. Having been the first born, the feeling of rejection I experienced when he was born was nearly unbearable to me. I felt anger about this, which I did not want anyone to know about (even myself), and I kept a relatively tight lid on it, but what was really there was a well of grief.

I wrote, "I'm a tough nut to crack. I will not open, I don't want to, it's hard being vulnerable. I just get hurt anyway." But who was I hurting when I did that?

My friend Peggy Black wrote,

"Human beings long ago learned to close or protect their heart circuit. This is the main dysfunction on your planet and the main source of dis-ease. There are wounds passed down from generation to generation. These programs/beliefs close and numb your responses to the messages and guidance coming from and going to this heart center." (Peggy Black, *Morning Messages*, 2010, pg. 182.)

"When the heart is energetically closed to others, it is closed to the divine. It is time that humanity heals the wounded heart." (Black, *Morning Messages*, 2010, pg. 80.)

So when the birds came, I knew they came for me and I felt cared for, loved and full. They brought me a message too, and the message was: "The truth will set you free."

What was the truth? It was time to admit that I felt lonely and rejected. I had to admit it instead of stuffing it and remaining tight and protected. I had to feel the grief with compassion for myself. I had to let go of being angry with myself about my anger!

"So look and see where you can soften and release some of the old patterns, some of the toxic emotions that you carry…Now is the time to consciously…with a gentle heart…love yourself free of limitation… We invite you to stay in your heart and bring anything that is not balanced, anything that is toxic, and anything that is limiting into your heart for total alchemical transformation. Your heart is a chalice for transformation. You are truly powerful alchemists. We know that when you decide to use the awesome tools available for transformation, you will shine like the most radiant star in the galaxy." (Black, *Morning Messages*, 2010, pg. 87)

I thought I was going to fill the center circle with dried pink rose petals. The center had been empty through the whole process, empty and blank and waiting. But when I got to the hour of placing the petals, they weren't right. I placed one rosebud at the center and it was finished. I felt pleased. I loved the birds which had come to me with their songs of love and their message. I loved being in the wonderful energy they brought which pervaded my being all the days I worked on the painting. I loved the dried rose leaves I placed in the painting—I even enhanced them with green watercolor when they started to turn brown. And, I especially loved the pink rosebud floating at the center, at the heart. Does it wait in the circle in the center for something? I think it does.

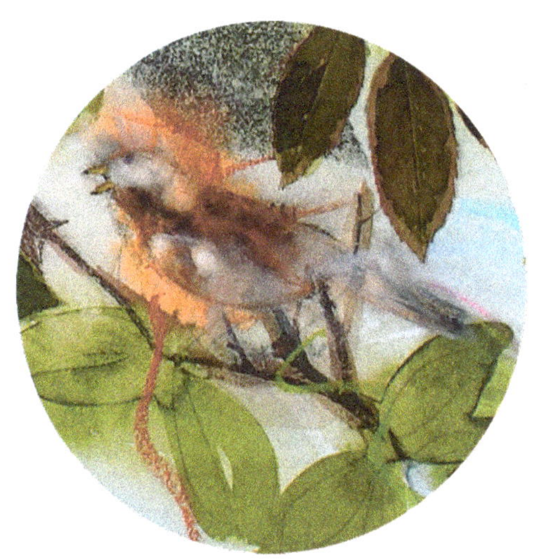

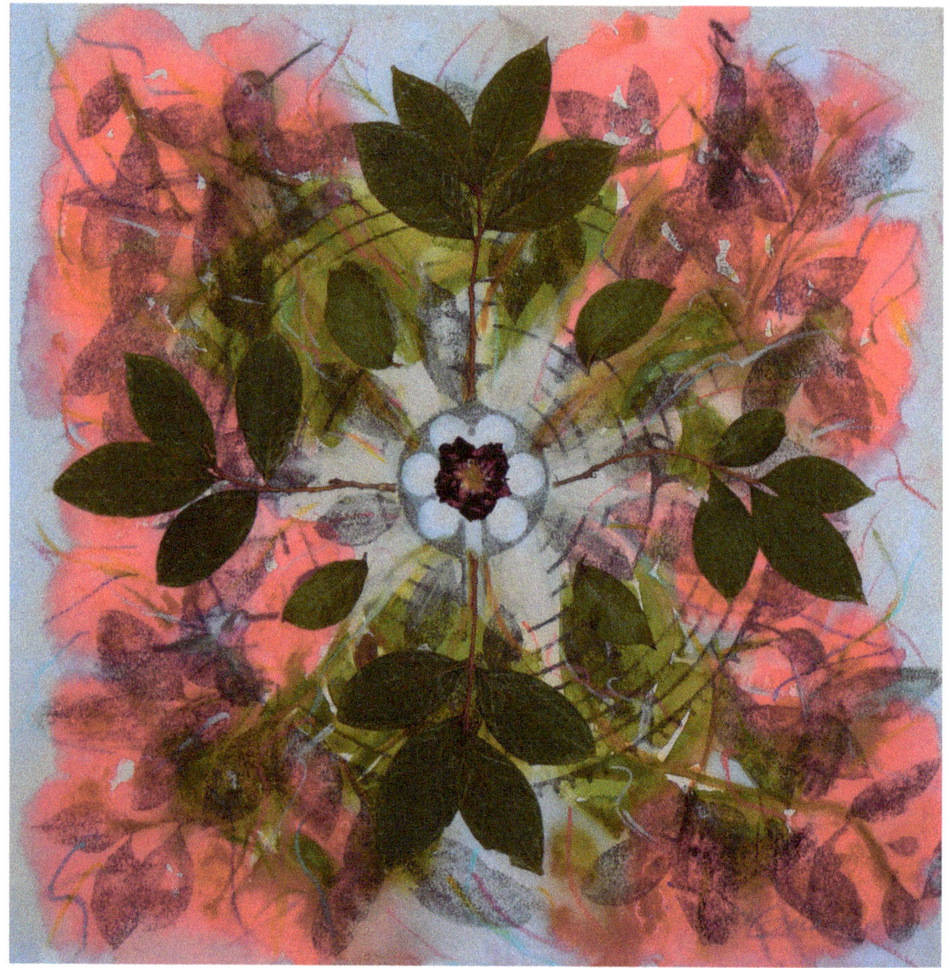

"Follow The Path To The Divine Feminine"

Ink transfer, watercolor, gouache, colored pencil, oil pastel, dried rose and leaves, 15" x 15" 2011

A Messenger Of The Highest Order

I had to go for my annual physical at a clinic out of town. I decided that after I was finished with all the tests, I would, by way of heading home, go find the labyrinth I had heard about (the story in Mandala Twelve, pg. 111) and walk it. I Googled its location and found it fairly easily. It was a labyrinth based on the one from the floor of Chartres Cathedral in France, a church dedicated to the Virgin Mary.

No one was around when I got to the labyrinth. It was located outdoors as you approached an Episcopal church. Its perfect design in black was laid out on rust-colored cement and looked very beautiful. I began to walk it quickly. I'd spent way too much time with doctors and exams, and was getting irritable and wanted to get home.

Besides, it was hot that day and I wanted to get out of the sun and into the shade.

As I started walking, I stopped myself and thought, "That's not the way to walk a labyrinth!" There was a voice inside, however, which didn't agree and wanted to "hurry up."

But, I started over. I took a step and stopped, and then another, and stopped. Somewhere among the curves and turns I forgot about the uncomfortable heat and my irritability. As I finished walking into the labyrinth and out, I seemed to float and felt centered, calm and blissful. I got in my car and headed home. The road over the mountain was narrow and windy and I came around a blind curve to find a driver in my lane, heading straight for me passing a car in his lane. There was nowhere for me to go to avoid him. I really do not know how we missed hitting head-on, but when the moment passed and I was safe, I started to cry in shock. Then I realized I had been protected, and without a doubt, it was Our Lady, the divine feminine.

I knew I would do a mandala commemorating this powerful experience. Thus this painting, *Follow the Path to the Divine Feminine.* The base, or background design, is the Chartres Cathedral labyrinth. The flowers are crepe myrtle which were blooming everywhere in the town that had the labyrinth. I placed dried leaves in the painting from a crepe myrtle tree. I left the center open after I finished the piece, waiting for what? Or was it to remain empty? The center of this particular labyrinth design is called a rose. Soon I knew I wanted a real rose in the middle, and the rose I chose was an open and fully bloomed dried red rose. I didn't really notice or think about the difference between it and the rose bud in *The Birds Came* until I wrote this. The first was a closed rose bud, and the second was bloomed and open. I felt good about the fully blooming nature of this rose. It seemed symbolic of being open to all these experiences which were happening to me. What were these experiences' common denominator? The Virgin Mary, the Mother of God, the divine feminine. She's following me, helping me, loving me, caring for me. She is a messenger of the highest order! I finally thought I was finished with the mandala. But I wasn't. Some hummingbirds flew into the picture. Where did they come from? Well, why wouldn't they want to drink the nectar available there?

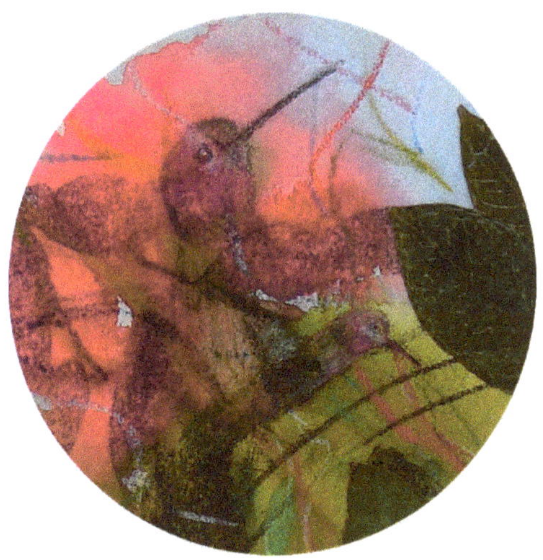

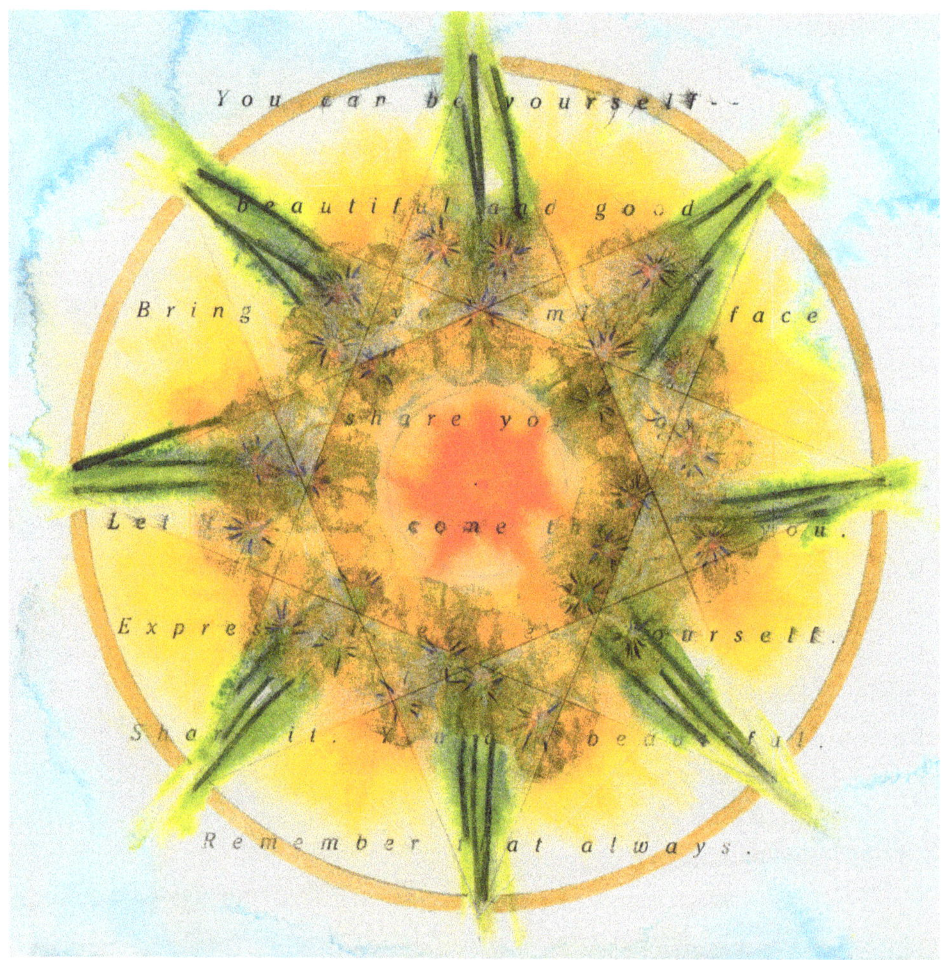

ABOUT THE PAINTING

"YOU CAN BE YOURSELF: MESSAGE FROM MY WHEEL OF LIFE"

Ink transfer, watercolor, gouache, colored pencil, oil pastel, 8.5"x 8.5" 2012

FLOWERS ARE LOVE AND LOVE HEALS ALL

I was seeing bouquets of yellow violas which appeared to be a gift for me. Why the violas?

I had been on my case for dragging my feet about updating my website. I had planned on selling prints of my work on the web for a couple of years, but never got to it. I was pushing myself to no avail. And then I realized I was scared, or more correctly, traumatized. I was experiencing that old fear of being exposed and vulnerable and I wanted to hide. When I was young at school, I really liked Show & Tell and probably bored the kids silly with my daily sharing. I talked about everything and I soon learned that was not OK, especially telling about family matters. So after having to go back to school and apologize for what I had said, I stopped. I bit my lip, sucked it up, got quiet and depressed. I was a talker—but I stopped and tried to become invisible.

I felt the violas were coming to me to give me a new life's message. This was the message and I put it in the center of the painting: You can be yourself, beautiful and good. Bring out your smiling face and share your joy, let the joy come through you. Express it, Express yourself. Share it. You are beautiful. Remember that always.

The violas were so sweet and cheery and I wanted to sit with them and their magical smiling faces in my garden.

I contemplated the painting before I started it and determined to do a wheel of life with eight spokes and eight bouquets of violas. A wheel of life is a representation of how you live your life—the different aspects of it divided in a circle—home, work, health, etc.

As I sat with the violas, I saw that they were blooming more abundantly than I'd ever seen. Excited, I listened.

Don't worry. Be happy! Everything is perfect just the way it is. We are with you, we care as you can never know. Bloom as they are. Full, beautifully and completely full out. You can be yourself. The world needs you to be yourself. Thank you for coming out and sitting with us. Know we are here. Know we know you. Know we are here for you. Realize we are connected to you in spirit. Know that all the flowers are. What is the message each has for you? Maybe you ought to ask...and then listen. Enter our world. It is most beautiful, as are you. You are welcome. Come in. Don't be shy. Walk in. Be with us now. In your brightness, with your spirit, with your smiles, with your joy. We feel it. Let others feel it. Let it out to the world. Be our voice and speak to others of our joy, the joy the flowers have in blooming. The joy of life—of being alive, of being who they are. Show yourself. Be who you are. Bring the message to all, the nature of flowers—their message, their messages to all. Ask us. We will tell you and not keep our message a secret. Try it, you'll like it. And take heed. We have much to say, much we want to share with you. We hold old, deep wisdom and are ready to share it. Will you listen? Will you connect with us? Will you receive our love? Will you take this love and share it? It will heal the world. Will you take just one flower and imbibe its heady nectar, commune deeply with it and share what you have been given? How has it touched you? How has it healed you and given you new life? Will you? You will get more than you bargained for. It's powerful. Watch out. You may change and overflow with its nectar and essence. And when the two of you are gathered in the name of love, what new has now been created? It's a miracle. Take a moment, you'll see. Your heart will overflow with gratitude, and you'll wonder if you really have ever had your eyes open, or your heart. Flowers are love, just pure love. And love heals all! Want to go on a magical journey? Pick a flower, any flower. And watch the miracle unfold. Will you then pick a flower and give it to someone? What a gift. A new self can emerge. Is this the truth, you wonder? What have you got to lose? Find that flower, bend over and be filled with its fragrant essence and begin your journey of gratitude, appreciation and joy.

Oh! You have told me much, my dear violas.

You came and you stopped a moment and you asked. What more could one ask for?

Thank you.

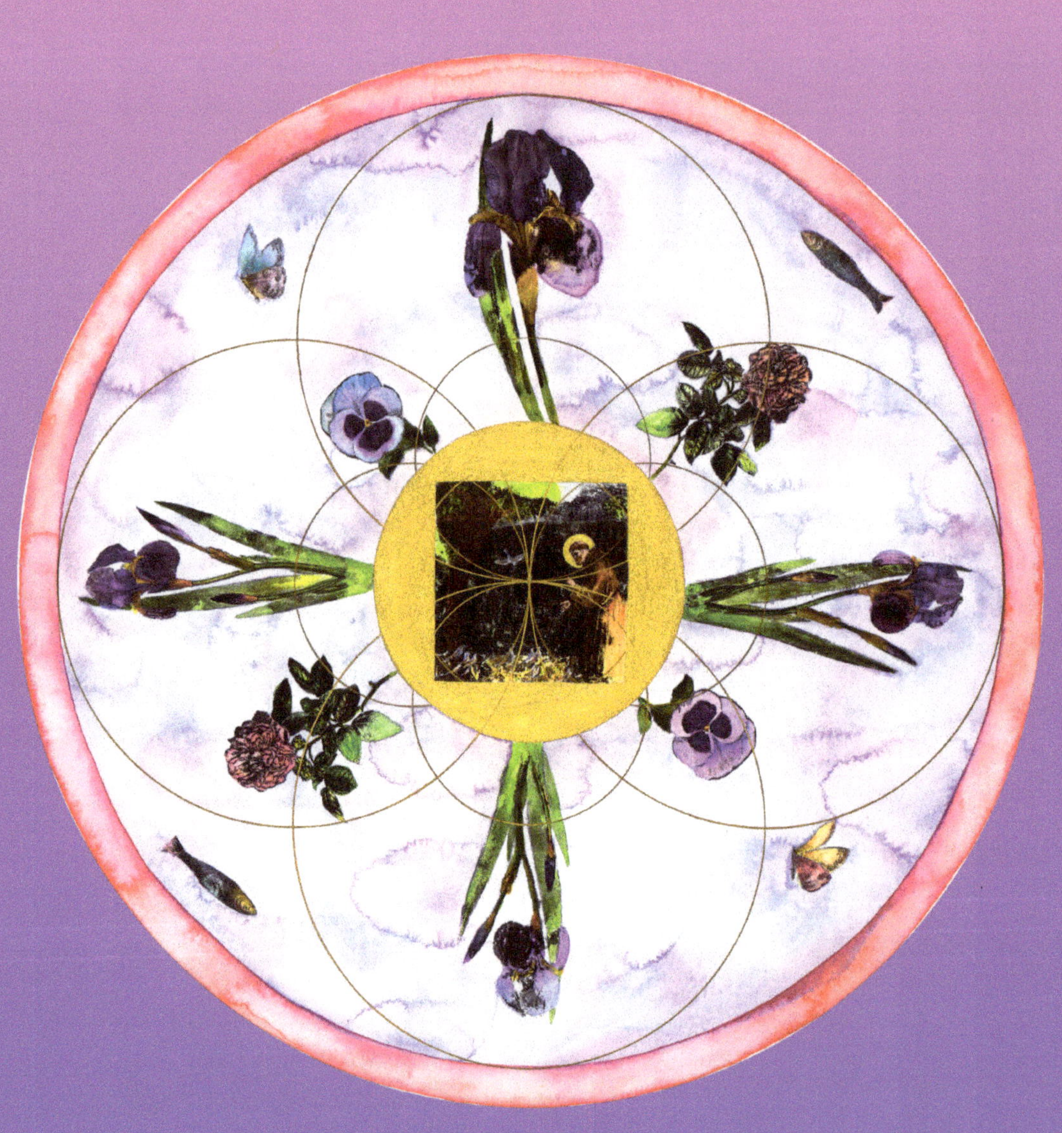

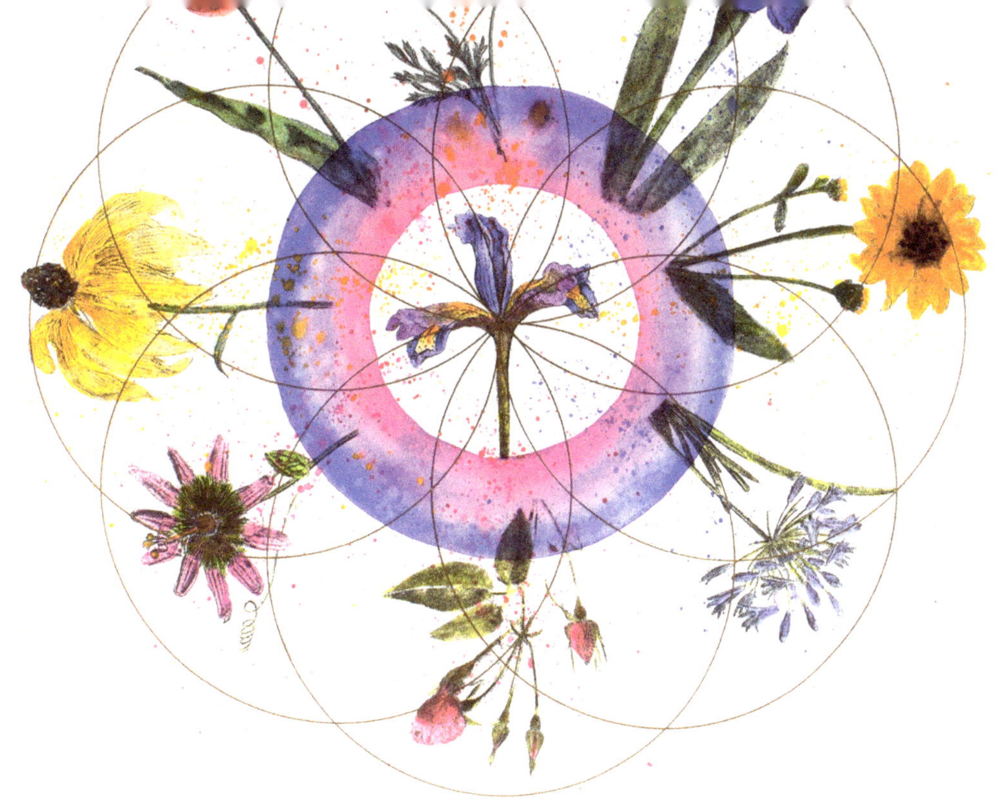

The Real Adventure Begins

THE CONCLUSION
And A Message from St. Germaine
February 25, 2015

While messages and words had come from spirit as far back as the late 1980s, it wasn't until 2000 that I received the first message from St. Germaine telling me we were going to write a book together. I thought I'd completed the book in late 2001. But the book sat for many years until I realized there was going to be another part, since so much had transpired in those years in between. And, so I began to write Part V with the chosen mandalas. It brought up some fear which I was not expecting! I put the book back on the shelf. I have heard it said that the thing that scares you the most is the thing that you came to do.

In 2014, with Part V having been completed for some months, I took the book off the shelf again and began to edit with a new laptop, a new program, and the data all transferred to a new system. I was ready to take the next step toward making this a real book.

But what was interesting, was that as I completed the edit, and re-read the whole manuscript, I began to feel a new sense of self from within. The words weren't falling on my own deaf ears. I believed the words more and more and did not push them away. I began embracing them and accepting who I was. That seemed to be the whole point of the book—transforming from a person who was full of self-doubt to one who could accept her self-worth. It was not easy sloughing off that old skin, but it has now been done and I can accept the me that I was all along. My guides, guardians and the All That Is has had such infinite patience. I'm glad they believed in me and did not give up.

Years later when I re-read my guides' words, I found them to be as fresh, poignant, spiritually powerful and loving as the moment I "heard" them. That still amazes me. What St. Germaine called my "true work," has opened my heart to a deeper, profound connection with spirit. I have become strong through light and color. My gratitude is without words.

My guides said that there would be an "awakening." But how it would unfold and what it would look like I didn't know. I'm just glad I said yes to it and took the steps as they were presented, even though there were definitely times I wanted to turn over and go back to sleep. From the beginning, what my guides told me was going to happen, and what happened, was consistent and never changed. I trusted and followed the guidance I was given and as I came to the end of the experience and the book, I knew that there had been, as they said there would be, a "shift" and a "new life created."

Everything you have read is the truth, and all of it happened to me just as I wrote it.

My friend Lee Carroll said this:

"The puzzle during your life is about how much of this truth of being part of the Creator you can accept. How far can you open the quantum door to see this truth…" (Lee Carroll, *Kryon; The Recalibration of Humanity,* 2013, pg. 236.)

With my heart full of love and infinite colors, I go forward. I invite you to journey with me, reader, to fill your heart with light and color and watch the transformation and the sparks fly— for they surely will. Thank you for staying the course and finishing with me. And remember what St. Francis said:

When you heal your earth body, through the work with the colors, then you will heal your spirit body. And when you heal your spirit body, you may enter into the realm of the divine cosmos and flow with all love, all harmony, all unity. This will open you to such joy you have never known, and this is where the real adventures begin.

Before I concluded I asked St. Germaine for help. "St. Germaine, can you give me words—a message for the Conclusion of Book II?"

I am happy that we can meet again in this way of communication and I am overjoyed to give you, and all, a message for the conclusion of this very special project. We have been with you all along, and yes, we will never leave you. But this is a special occasion for the conclusion of a most divine and guided book with words and art work that came from on high.

We are so proud and pleased with your progress, both on the project but most assuredly on your growth and the stepping into your new being-ness. The road was long and sometimes hard, very hard, and we know of your darkness and struggles which overcame you at times. But you pursued, stepping forth bravely through the fear, unsureness, and all the myriad of emotions that washed up. You have become strong and are becoming stronger and traveling down the avenue of worthiness. You know it and you feel it. We thank you for reaching out your hand for assistance from us on your travels and in your times of questioning and uncertainty. We were and are always available for help. You have become bright and beautiful as you accept and wear the mantle of spirit. It becomes you.

Yours has truly been a rebirth in Spirit and we have waited for this day. We smile brightly as you do, as you carry the joy of the loving heart of the Creator in you. We know you are pleased as well, for now you understand what we have expressed to you for a long time. But the time is here now and you will, and are, going forth in Spirit. You have awakened to know who you are and that is Spirit and a true child of God. We feel you relaxing into it and smile as your heart opens wider with love.

The Book project we started together is nearly finished and it will soon be open for the world to see. Your work is everyone's work. It is a grand project and has the greatest end ever—the birth in Spirit. You have completed it well and fulfilled our commitment for the work together. You didn't know where it was going, or when it would conclude. Do you understand now? It concluded with your awakening. You thought those were just words at first, we think.

But now your experience is that it is true and you have lived it. The bursting forth from your cocoon is a good metaphor, for now you can leave your small self and spread your wings. As we said before, now the adventure really begins.

We are always with you and await our new work together. Call on us anytime, anywhere.

In deepest love, joy and gratitude,
Your guide and partner,
St. Germaine
and All

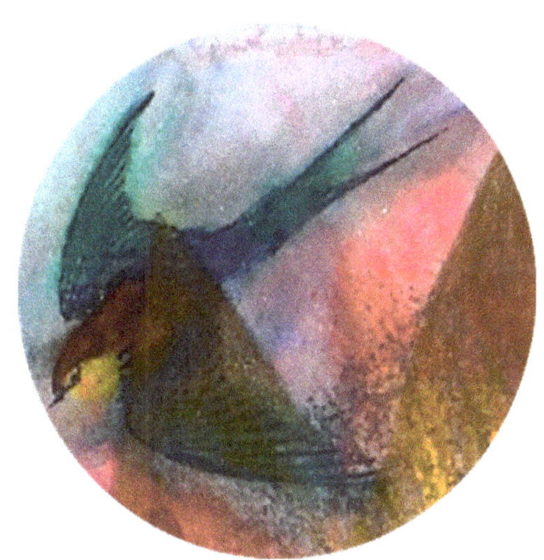

Acknowledgements

No one is more deserving of thanks than my husband. I would not be the artist I have become without his belief in me. In addition to his encouragement and unending support, he is an amazing designer and has done an awesome job of designing this book. His love has changed my life.

Thank you to our dear friend and colleague Bonno Bernard for her design skills, special touches and patience in formatting this from an e-book to a real, hold-in-your-hands book. Thank you to my son-in-law's mother Jan Gollaher, who volunteered her editing skills. As she edited, she cheered me on, believing in me and savoring the messages, having been a receiver of messages herself. How we were brought together by our children is such a beautiful example of spirit working. A huge thank you goes to Elaine Rivas, my amazing friend, who offered to do proofreading. She was invaluable.

Once again I must thank my parents: my mother for her love of flowers and color, and my father who taught me the love of growing a garden. At 90 they both continue to garden, my dad growing their vegetables and my mom caring for her flowers. I am SO grateful!

Thank you to one of the most beautiful human beings I have ever met, my daughter Denise Gollaher. And another thank you to her for her gift of my granddaughter, Megan Gollaher. For all of the unknown gifts of love they have given me, thank you.

I must thank Maggie Cheney for a second time. She nudged me so many years ago into writing my first book, and then again for this one. Many thanks go to therapist Joanne Young for believing in me, in my art, and helping me through the difficult times. Her kindness, support and gentleness helped me be brave as I healed my own self-doubt.

Thank you to all my friends and guides in spirit who have been with me through this journey. The writing of this book was an endeavor of trust, faith and believing in the unseen. My teachers in spirit were always there. The late Hope Naylor is probably one of those precious beings on the other side who, while she was alive, believed in me as a light-worker and a channeler. And now years later, I am teaching the daughter of one of our fellow students from her class. The teachings have come full circle! Therefore, my gratitude would not be complete without mentioning my spiritual sister Carol Bellandi, who introduced me to Hope Naylor. Thank you!

About The Author

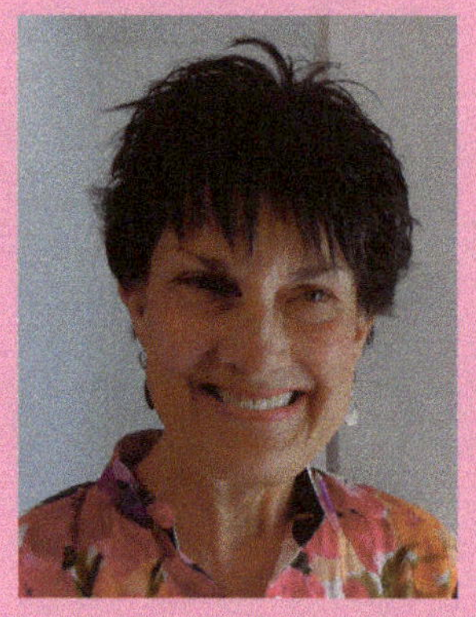

Michele Faia has been painting and teaching for over 30 years. She holds bachelor and master's degrees in art history. She lives on the coast of Central California with her husband who is also an artist. She is currently teaching watercolor mandala classes locally and workshops in the United States. See more about her work on her website www.michelefaia.com and an in-depth biography with photos at www.michelefaia.com/bio/.